WRITING WITH LOGIC

Mastering 15 Patterns of Development in Writing

15の論理展開パターンで攻略する

英文ライティング

石井洋佑
Yosuke Ishii

日本能率協会マネジメントセンター

本書の内容に関するお問い合わせについて

平素は日本能率協会マネジメントセンターの書籍をご利用いただき、ありがとうございます。

弊社では、皆様からのお問い合わせへ適切に対応させていただくため、以下①～④のようにご案内しております。

① お問い合わせ前のご案内について

現在刊行している書籍において、すでに判明している追加・訂正情報を、弊社の下記 Web サイトでご案内しておりますのでご確認ください。

https://www.jmam.co.jp/pub/additional/

②ご質問いただく方法について

①をご覧いただきましても解決しなかった場合には、お手数ですが弊社 Web サイトの「お問い合わせフォーム」をご利用ください。ご利用の際はメールアドレスが必要となります。

https://www.jmam.co.jp/inquiry/form.php

なお、インターネットをご利用ではない場合は、郵便にて下記の宛先までお問い合わせください。電話、FAX でのご質問はお受けしておりません。

〈住所〉 〒103-6009　東京都中央区日本橋 2-7-1　東京日本橋タワー 9F

〈宛先〉 ㈱日本能率協会マネジメントセンター　ラーニングパブリッシング本部　出版部

③ 回答について

回答は、ご質問いただいた方法によってご返事申し上げます。ご質問の内容によっては弊社での検証や、さらに外部へお問い合わせすることがございますので、その場合にはお時間をいただきます。

④ ご質問の内容について

おそれいりますが、本書の内容に無関係あるいは内容を超えた事柄、お尋ねの際に記述箇所を特定されないもの、読者固有の環境に起因する問題などのご質問にはお答えできません。資格・検定そのものや試験制度等に関する情報は、各運営団体へお問い合わせください。

また、著者・出版社のいずれも、本書のご利用に対して何らかの保証をするものではなく、本書をお使いの結果について責任を負いかねます。予めご了承ください。

　英語の知識に自信はあっても，ライティングが苦手だという人はたくさんいます．処方箋は簡単です．ライティングができない理由は次の 2 つのうちのいずれか，あるいは両方と決まっているからです．

　　① 書く練習をしていない
　　② 学習の方向性が間違っている

　実はライティングのテキストは，洋書ではよいものがたくさんあります．和書でも，表現を扱うものでは，昔から﨑村耕二さんが『英語で明確に説明する 基礎編』（創元社），『論理的な英語が書ける本』（大修館書店）など一連の本を出されています．ネットで話題となり復刊された長谷三郎さんの『伝わる英語表現法』（岩波新書）もあります．近年では鈴木健士さんの『ここで差がつく！ 英文ライティングの技術』（テイエス企画）があります．論理・構成面を扱う好著にはケリー伊藤さんの『英語パラグラフ・ライティング講座』（研究社）や津田塾大学英文学科編の『パラグラフから始める英文ライティング入門』（研究社）などがあります．近年出版されたものでは津島玲子さんの『究極の英語ライティングBasic』（アルク）や井上逸兵さんの『もっともシンプルな英語ライティング講義』（慶應義塾大学出版会）に構成の基本がコンパクトにまとまっています．2023年には『ゼロから覚醒 はじめよう英作文』（かんき出版）という初学者向けの自分の本も出ています．

　しかし，優れたテキストを読んでなるほどなあと感心しても，ライティング力は上達しません．手を動かして自分で英語を書いてみて，それをじっくり観察して必要があれば直す，という作業が必要です．ところが残念ながら，そういう作業をしてみようという人はあまりいないようです．なぜ自分で書かないのかとたずねると，「まだ自分は文法力や語彙力が足りないから」とほとんどの人が答えます．文法や語彙の力を伸ばすのはよいことですが，自分の現在の英語力で

いかに相手に通じるための表現や構成のスキルを身につけることはもっと大事です. なぜなら, 日本語であれ英語であれ, 相手にわかってもらうために書くのであり, 自分が「イケてる」英語が使えることを見せつけるためではないからです. 本書で扱うセンテンスの作り方・つなげ方・まとめ方を身につければ, 中学英語程度の文法や語彙でも伝わる文章を書くのは十分に可能です.

　本書のテーマはたった1つです.「センテンスを与えられたら, それにつながる別のセンテンスを書けるようにする」. このたった1つのことができるようになればライティングはずいぶん楽になります. 類書には見られない量の実際に書いてみるタスクが本書には入っています. スポーツに例えれば, 実戦での状況・場面を意識した練習です. 基礎体力をつけるトレーニングと練習試合ばかりやっても, 野球でもサッカーでもバスケットボールでも, うまくはなりません. 展開パターンをマスターするには, 手を動かして自分なりの解答を作り, 参考解答と比べながら何度も書き直す作業を続けてください. 本書を終えるころには英語の論理に沿って文章を構成する力が十分についているはずです.

　「センテンスを提示して, それにつなげるセンテンスを書くタスクを入れる」というアイディアは松井恵美子さん（戸板女子短期大学准教授）と話をしていたときに出たものです. 当時は, 一緒に初級者向けに大学教科書を出すことを考えていましたが, 対象を変え, 一般語学書にそのアイディアを生かすことにしました. 本書がライティング学習者の一助となることを願ってやみません. 最後に, DHC社からの版権移行と改訂版の編集をスピーディーに行なって下さった, 日本能率協会マネジメントセンターラーニングパブリッシング本部出版部出版コンテンツ開発センター長の山地淳さん, 担当の竹田恵さんに感謝を申し上げます.

2024年3月　Yosuke Ishii

本書は2023年に刊行された『英文を編む技術』(石井洋佑 著、株式会社DHC) を基に、Sample Answersへの別解の追加、解説の追加などを行い、改訂したものです。

Chapter 3 │ 文章をまとめる　⟨161⟩

　本書は Chapter 1 〜 3 の三部構成になっています．各チャプターでの学習方法は次の通りです．

Chapter 1 の学習方法

- ライティングに使えるシンプルな例文を 100 に絞り込んで掲載しています．
- 左ページに英語の例文，右ページに和訳を掲載し，ページ下部に註釈（学習者にありがちなミスや疑問点の解説）を掲載しています．
- 例文の意味がわかるかどうかを確認したうえで，まだ使いこなせていないと感じるセンテンスはぜひ頭に入れてください．

Chapter 2 の学習方法

- 最初のセンテンスから次のセンテンスにどうつなげていくか，その展開パターンを 15 に厳選して掲載しています．
- まずは展開パターンについての解説を読み，穴埋めタイプの確認問題（Let's practice!）で理解を深めましょう．
- その後，Exercise に取り組みます．Exercise では，必ず自分なりの解答を作ってから Sample Answers を確認してください．
- ＊ 確認問題（Let's practice!）がない構成のセクションもあります．

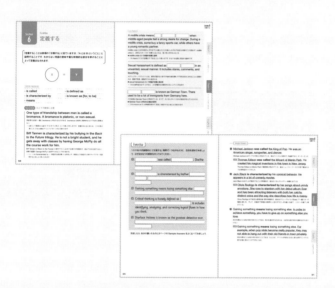

Chapter 3 の学習方法

- 本書の総まとめとして，IELTS と TOEFL 形式のライティング問題を掲載しています.

- 問題文を読み，構成を考えてからエッセイを書いてみましょう.

- 辞書を引かずに，今の自分の英語力で書き上げることが大切です. その後で Sample Answer を読んでポイントを確認してください.

Chapter 1

センテンスを
組み立てる

最初にライティングをするにあたって，最低限使え
るようにしておきたいセンテンスパターンに取り組
みましょう．ごく普通のシンプルな表現だけを 100
厳選しました.
ぜひ，この 100 例文を使いこなせるようにインプッ
トしていきましょう.

Writing clear sentences

わかりやすいセンテンスとは

> まとまった量のライティングも，結局はセンテンスの組み合わせです．したがって，センテンスが書けないと何も始まりません．センテンスを組み立てる上である程度の文法の知識は必要ですが，ライティングは複雑な文法事項を習得しているかどうかを競うコンテストではありません．相手に伝えるために，ひとつひとつのセンテンスを組み立てていけばいいのです．

わかりやすいセンテンスというのは，トピック（そのセンテンスが何についてのものか）とコメント（トピックがどうするのか／どうなのか）が明確になっているものです．

▶ **Learning new things is important.**

トピック　　　　　　　　　コメント

新しいことを学ぶことは大切だ．

▶ **High school teachers need more time to develop their**

トピック　　　　　　　　コメント

subject area knowledge and teaching skills.

高校の先生は，教科の知識や教授技術を伸ばすための時間がもっと必要だ．

通常の場合，トピックはセンテンスの **S**（subject: 主語／主部）であり，コメントは V（verb: 動詞部分）から続く **P**（pradicate：述部）と一致しますが，次のような場合もあります．

▶ **In Okinawa, it rarely snows.**

トピック　　　　　　コメント

沖縄では雪はほとんど降らない．

▶ **In today's world, there are so many conflicts**

トピック　　　　　　　　　　コメント

between nations, cultures, and religions.

今日の世界では，国家間，文化間，宗教間においてたくさんの争いがある．

　自分のいいたいことをトピック＋コメントの構造に落とし込むには，基本的なセンテンスのパターンが頭に入っている必要があります．しかし，そのための適切な教材はありません．世の教材は，シンプルな英語でセンテンスを組み立てる学習者をターゲットにしたものではないからです．「構文集」は，読む際に知らないと理解が難しい複雑な文構造のセンテンスを集めたものです．和文英訳用の受験用参考書は，日本語と英語の発想の違いからミスを犯しやすい文構造や語法を押さえるためのものです．「瞬間英作文」の教材は，口頭でのアウトプット用のセンテンスの文構造を体に叩き込むためのものです．ネイティヴが使う自然な慣用表現をまとめたものは素朴な英語を重ねてメッセージを伝えることができるようになった学習者がターゲットです．そこで，Chapter 1 では，最低限使えるようにしておきたいセンテンスパターンを 100 にまとめました．ネイティヴらしい慣用表現や受験用頻出表現ではなくネイティヴにとってもノンネイティヴにとってもごくごく普通の表現だけ選びました．学習者にありがちなミスや疑問点には註をつけました．

　英語が得意な人は飛ばすか，サッと目を通した後，すぐに Chapter 2 に進んで構いません．ただ，自信をもって書いた英語に「そんな小難しい表現を使わずに，もっとシンプルでいいのに」といったダメ出しを受けた経験がある人は，この 100 センテンスのように表現することを意識するとよいでしょう．センテンスパターンのストックが足りないと感じている人は，例文の意味がわかるかどうか確認した上で，このパターンでオリジナルのセンテンスを作れないと思うものを覚えてください．身についたかどうかの判断が難しいときは，和訳だけを見てサッと元の英語を言う練習をするとよいでしょう．少し時間がかかるかもしれませんが，100 パターン全部覚えるとライティングの際に個々のセンテンスをひねり出すのに苦労することが減り，論理構成や読ませるための工夫に意識を向けることができるようになります．

　学習者は「文法に自信がないからライティングの勉強はまだ始められない」という思考に陥りがちです．しかし，TOEFL や IELTS のような英語試験のライティング答案でさえ，大半のセンテンスはこの 100 パターンで構成されています．まずは，この 100 パターンをしっかりマスターすることに集中してみてはどうでしょうか．

100 common sentence patterns for writing well

ライティングに使える！
英文パターン 100

① Honesty pays.

② Tastes differ.

③ Studying comes first.

④ Kenji always causes trouble.

⑤ Jody's attitude makes me mad.

⑥ Bonnie dyed her hair pink.

⑦ Danny is considered a troublemaker.

⑧ Jerry fixed the broken window.

⑨ Jessica hardly knew the suspect.

⑩ I ate spaghetti for dinner yesterday.

「トピック+コメント」と「意味順」

Who (だれが)	Does/Is (する／です)	Whom/What (だれ／なに)	Where (どこ)	When (いつ)
Honesty	pays.			
トピック	コメント			

Section 1で示した トピック ＋ コメント ＝ センテンス という枠組みはそのまま，名古屋外国語大学の田地野彰教授が提唱する意味順モデルにあてはまります．ただし，会話では Who (だ

---

1. 学校英語では Honesty is the best policy. と習うかもしれないが，実用ではこちらの方がよく使われる．皮肉屋は Honesty doesn't pay. ということも． 2. 受験で習う There is no accounting for taste. よりもこちらの方が普通かつ使いやすい． 3. = Studying is the most important. 4. 「起こす」と「起きる」の区別が付かず，✗ Kenji always occurs trouble. のようなミスをする学習者が多い．raise/rise なども注意しよう． 5. make 人／もの・こと 状態「人／もの・ことを状態にする」．

❶　正直者は報われる.

❷　人の好みはさまざまだ.

❸　学業が最優先だ.

❹　Kenji はいつも問題を起こす.

❺　Jody の態度は頭にくる.

❻　Bonnie は彼女の髪の毛をピンクに染めた.

❼　Danny はトラブルメーカーと考えられている.

❽　Jerry は壊れた窓を直した.

❾　Jessica はその容疑者のことをほとんど知らなかった.

🔟　昨日は，晩ごはんはスパゲッティを食べた.

れが）に入るトピックは単語はほとんどが人ですが，ライティングでは honesty「正直であること」のようなもの（具体的な物質・物体）やこと（抽象的な概念）がトピックになり，対応するpay「（もの・ことが）割に合う」（「（金額を）支払う」ではない）のような動詞でコメントが始まることもあります.「意味順」を意識しながら，基本的な動詞の用法に習熟することが必要になります.（意味順モデルについては『「意味順」で学ぶ英会話』(JMAM) などを参照してください）

---

6. Hiroshi likes his coffee black.「Hiroshi はコーヒーをブラックと決めている」など,「動詞 もの・こと 状態」というシンプルな表現パターンを知っていると便利.　7. consider 人 役割「人を役割と考える」の受け身. is considered to be a troublemaker は可だが, ✕ is considered as a troublemaker は非一般的.　8. -ed/en 形が名詞の前で形容詞の働き.　9. Rob studied hard (✕ hardly) yesterday.「Rob は昨日一生懸命勉強した」10.「昨日は」に引きずられて ✕ Yesterday ate spaghetti... / ✕ Yesterday is spaghetti... などとしないように.

⑪ Nao looked satisfied with the explanation.

⑫ The idea Tim suggested sounds innovative.

⑬ The movie starts at 6:20 P.M.

⑭ Hannah felt she was in danger.

⑮ Jennifer asked for toast with butter.

⑯ PJ works as much as Catherine.

⑰ Everybody regards me as Linda's best friend.

⑱ Akane can make herself understood in English.

⑲ Mr. Yoshinari got the computer working again.

⑳ Saki works part-time at a grocery store.

| to *do* |

　センテンスをつくるには「意味順」と動詞の用法に馴染むのが基本だと前ページで述べました. 次に大事なことは動詞の変化形である to *do*, *doing*, -ed/en の使い方です. ここではライティングのために押さえておくべき to *do* の典型的な用法とそれが使われている100パターンの例文番号を示します.

① to *do* が名詞のカタマリ → 42, 80, 83, 91

　to steal someone else's idea 「他の誰かの考えを盗むこと」(42)

② 〈動詞＋to *do*〉 → 43, 70, 92, 93

　decide to cancel the picnic 「そのピクニックを中止することに決める」(43)

---

11. Nao was satisfied with... と意味はほぼ同じだが, ライティングでは動詞に be を多用しない方がいい.
12. もの・こと look/sound/smell/feel/taste 形容詞.「もの・ことが形容詞のように見える／聴こえる／におう／感じる／味がする」13. ✗ The movie starts from 6:20 P.M. とするミスが多い.　14. ✗ Hannah felt she was dangerous. では「自分が危険人物だと感じた」になってしまう.　〇 Mr. Schmitt was in debt in those days.「Schmitt さんは当時借金を抱えていた」／ The building is on fire.「その建物に火災が発生中である」.

⑪ Nao はその説明に満足したようだった.

⑫ Tim が提案した案はとても斬新に思えた.

⑬ その映画の上映は午後 6 時 20 分に始まる.

⑭ Hannah は自分の身に危険が及んでいると感じた.

⑮ Jennifer はバターつきのトーストを頼んだ.

⑯ PJ は Catherine と同じぐらい働き者だ.

⑰ みんなは私を Linda の親友だと思っている.

⑱ Akane は英語で自分のいいたいことをわかってもらうことができる.

⑲ Yoshinari さんはコンピュータをまた動くようにした.

⑳ Saki はそのスーパーでバイトしている.

③ 〈動詞＋人＋ to *do*〉→ 37, 79, 81
get her husband to admit 「夫に認めさせる」(37)
　　　　　　　動作主

④ 〈名詞／代名詞＋ to *do*〉→ 29, 54, 67, 69
an obligation to pay taxes 「税金を払う義務」(54)

⑤ 動詞あるいはセンテンス全体にかかる目的・結果の to *do* → 78, 99
do whatever (to grow the economy) 「経済を成長させるためには何でもする」(99)

15. toast <u>with butter</u> で名詞のカタマリ.　16. = ... as much as Catherine does.　17. regard 人／もの・こと as 属性「人／もの・ことを属性と見なす」.　18. make yourself understood = express yourself　19. get もの・こと *doing*「もの・ことが……するようにさせる」.(→ 37)　20. have a part-time job「バイトがある」は知っていても work part-time「バイトをする，バイトで働く」とサクッと表現できる学習者は少ない.

㉑ Mia hardly ever goes out to lunch.

㉒ Eli is too young to get married.

㉓ You can't always get what you want.

㉔ Whatever happens, I will be with you.

㉕ Most people at work call Mr. Armstrong Andrew.

㉖ Jason seems to know a lot of things.

㉗ People under considerable stress sometimes make horrible mistakes.

㉘ We often go shopping in Shibuya after school.

㉙ Nobody knew what to do at the moment.

㉚ Mike was chosen as our leader after discussion.

| doing |

doing の押さえておくべき用法とそれが使われている 100 パターンの例文番号を示します.
④については 100 パターンの中に使用例がないので,例をここにあげます.

① doing が名詞のカタマリ → 3, 40, 41, 63, 97
analyzing things「物事を分析すること」(63)

② 〈動詞＋ doing〉 → 28, 37, 58, 59, 79
keep talking「話し続ける」

③ 〈動詞＋人＋ doing〉 → 19, 94
see Amanda and Harry having an argument
　　　　　　動作主
「Amanda と Harry が言い争いをしているところを見る」

---

21. = Mia seldom goes out to lunch. go out **to** lunch が慣用だが以下も可 : Mia hardly ever goes out **for** lunch. / Mia hardly ever **gets out to/for** lunch.　22. too ~ to do...「……するには〜すぎる」　23. what SV「S が……する／であるもの・こと」　24. whatever 動詞「何が……しても」　25. call/name 人 名前「人を名前と呼ぶ／名付ける」　26. seem to do...「……するように思える」.

㉑ Mia は昼食のために外食をすることはほとんどない.

㉒ Eli は結婚するには若すぎる.

㉓ 手に入れたいものはいつも手に入らない.

㉔ 何が起ころうと，君と一緒にいる.

㉕ 職場のほとんどの人は Armstrong さんを Andrew と呼ぶ.

㉖ Jason はたくさんのことを知っているように思える.

㉗ かなりのストレスを抱えている人はときどき大きな過ちを犯す.

㉘ 放課後，私たちはよく渋谷に買い物に行く.

㉙ 誰もそのときに何をすればよいのかわかっていなかった.

㉚ 話し合いの後，Mike が私たちのリーダーとして選ばれた.

④ 〈(限定詞＋) *do*ing ＋名詞〉
a missing person「失踪者」　boring jokes「つまらない冗談」
⑤ 〈(限定詞＋) 名詞＋ *do*ing ＋...〉→ 60
The women dancing in the street「通りで踊っている女性たち」(60)

27. People <u>under considerable stress</u> で名詞のカタマリ.　28. ✗ go to shopping　✗ go shopping to Shibuya　29. what to *do*「何をすべきか」，how to *do*「……する方法」，when to *do*「いつ……すべきか」，where to *do*「どこで……すべきか」30. choose 人 as 役職「人を役職に選ぶ」の受け身.

31 It appears that Wayne forgot our meeting today.

32 Matt hurt his left leg while playing soccer.

33 Oliver Stone creates movies that address social issues.

34 What Ms. Marcus says does not make sense.

35 We have a lot of rainy days in June.

36 A few people saw the man enter the room.

37 Karen got her husband to admit to his wrongdoing.

38 Some staff members helped clean up after the event.

39 The heiress kept her diamonds in a safe place.

40 My job that day was putting items on shelves.

| -ed/en |

-ed/en の典型的な用法とそれが使われている 100 パターンの例文番号を示します.

① 〈動詞＋ -ed/en〉 → 11, 46, 52, 75
get severely injured 「ひどい怪我を負わせる」

② 〈動詞＋人＋ -ed/en〉 → 18
make herself understood 「彼女自身を理解させる」
「人が…された」

---

31. it appears that ~ 「～ということらしい」(= apparently). 32. = Matt hurt his left leg while he was playing soccer. while/when SV = while doing 33. movies that address social issues 34. what SV 「S が……する／であるもの・こと」 35. A lot of rain falls in June. / There are a lot of rainy days in June. など とも表現できる.

31 Wayne は今日の会議を忘れたようだ.

32 Matt はサッカーをしている時, 左足にケガを負った.

33 Oliver Stone は社会問題を扱った映画を創る.

34 Marcus さんの言うことは意味をなさない.

35 6 月は雨の日が多い.

36 何人かの人がその男が部屋に入るのを見ている.

37 Karen は夫に彼の過ちを認めさせた.

38 何人かのスタッフが, 行事の後で掃除を手伝った.

39 その相続人は安全な場所にダイヤモンドを保管していた.

40 その日の私の仕事は商品の棚入れだ.

③ 〈〈限定詞＋〉-ed/en ＋名詞〉→ 8
the broken window 「その割れた窓」

④ 〈〈限定詞＋〉名詞 ＋ -ed/en ＋ ...〉→ 44, 71
the necklace left in the room 「部屋に残されたネックレス」

36. see 人 do は行動の一部始終を見る.　37. get, cause, force, allow など通常の「させる」系の動詞は get/cause/force/allow 人 to do. 例外は, have/let/help/make 人 do.　38. help do「……するのを手伝う」.
39. keep/put/leave/place... もの・こと 場所 「もの・ことを場所に置く」.　40. My job on that day... とするのは可だが, ✕ in this year とはしない：The Halloween event this year (✕ in this year) was fantastic.

41 Eating healthy food helps you stay in good shape.

42 It is totally wrong to steal someone else's idea.

43 We decided to cancel the picnic because of rain.

44 The necklace left in the room was not hers.

45 However hard you try, you can't be his girlfriend.

46 Fewer and fewer people get married in their 20s.

47 My dad gave me a teddy bear on my birthday.

48 We moved the desks and chairs to the conference room.

49 A lot of people are shocked by the president's remarks.

50 Most scientists agree that climate change is a serious issue.

---

41. *doing* の名詞用法.　42. ✘ To steal someone else's idea is totally wrong. のように to *do* を主語には通常しない.　43. decide to *do*, plan to *do*, choose to *do*, hope to *do*　44. -ed/en 形で始まる語句が名詞に後ろからかかっている.　45. however 状態 SV¹, SV². 「どんなに状態で SV¹ でも SV²」　46. = The number of people who get married in their 20s is decreasing.

㊶ 健康な食生活が体をよい状態に保つ.

㊷ ほかの誰かの考えを盗用するのは完全に間違っている.

㊸ 私たちは雨天のため, ピクニックを中止することにした.

㊹ 部屋に残されたネックレスは彼女のものではなかった.

㊺ どれだけ一生懸命やってみたところで, 君は彼の彼女にはなれないよ.

㊻ 20 代で結婚する人はどんどん減っている.

㊼ 父は誕生日にテディベアを買ってくれた.

㊽ 私たちは机と椅子を会議室に移動した.

㊾ 多くの人は社長の発言にショックを受けている.

㊿ 多くの科学者は気候変動が深刻な問題であると合意している.

---

47. give/teach 人 もの・こと = give/teach もの・こと to 人は中学で習う項目だが誤用しがち. 　48. move もの to/into 場所「ものを場所に動かす」, move to/into 場所「場所に移る」: We moved to the city. 　49. 受け身: 動作の受け手 be + -ed/en by 動作の主体　50. = Most scientists agree with the idea that...

51. The detective asked me whether I saw Jane last night.

52. Schneider got severely injured but could walk off the field.

53. Sayaka often spreads the news (that) she gets from her girlfriends.

54. Wherever you live, you have an obligation to pay taxes.

55. None of us believed that we could win the game.

56. Jenny waited for her boyfriend at the station for three hours.

57. Hitomi has been playing tennis since she was six years old.

58. Hiroshi enjoyed talking with different kinds of people after the event.

59. Two girls kept talking in the café for a few hours.

60. One of the women dancing in the street caught my attention.

---

51. whether ... 「……かどうか」. 52. but は got severely injured と could walk off the field という 2 つの動詞のカタマリをつないでいる. 53. the news (that) she gets from her girlfriends 54. wherever SV¹, SV² 「SV¹ はどこでも SV²」 55. ✗ All of us didn't believe... 56. wait for 人／もの・こと ✗ Jenny waited her boyfriend...

Chapter 1

センテンスを組み立てる

Chapter 2

センテンスをつなげる

Chapter 3

文章をまとめる

51 その刑事は私に昨晩 Jane に会ったかどうか尋ねた.

52 Schneider はひどい傷を負ったが，歩いて退場することができた.

53 Sayaka はよく女友達から聞いた情報を広めることがある.

54 どこに住もうと納税の義務はある.

55 私たちの中の誰もその試合に勝てるとは信じていなかった.

56 Jenny は駅で彼氏を 3 時間待った.

57 Hitomi は 6 歳の頃からテニスをずっと続けている.

58 Hiroshi はその行事の後，さまざまな人々と話をするのを楽しんだ.

59 2 人の女の子は数時間喫茶店で話し続けた.

60 通りで踊っていた女性の 1 人が私の注意を惹(ひ)いた.

---

57. since 過去の一時点 , for 期間 の使い分けに注意：Hitomi has been playing tennis for 15 years.
58. enjoy *doing*, finish *doing*, stop *doing*, mind *doing*, avoid *doing*, miss *doing*　59. keep (on) *doing*
「……し続ける」．　60. the women dancing in the street：*doing* 形が後ろから名詞を説明.

61. This YouTuber is known to a lot of people under 18.

62. Holmes told Inspector Lestrade that the case was not solved yet.

63. Nick is poor at analyzing things, but he shows great creativity.

64. Although cars are a good form of transportation, they harm the environment.

65. I was more nervous than I had thought I would be.

66. Lori told us her dirty little secret, which really shocked us.

67. The team did not have enough members to enter the tournament.

68. More and more women have positions of responsibility in Japanese companies.

69. Ms. Tsuchiya teaches college students how to study for the IELTS exam.

70. My boyfriend promised to take me to dinner at a French restaurant.

---

61. be known to 範囲「範囲に知られている」, be known as 役割「役割として知られている」, be known for 生産物「生産物で知られている」 62. tell 人 that ~「人に~ということを伝える」 63. 2つのセンテンスの間に but を挟むことで1つのセンテンスにしている。 64. SV¹, but SV². = Although SV¹, SV². = SV² although SV¹. 65. = I got more nervous than I (had) thought. 66. , which「そしてそれは」補足情報

61 このユーチューバーは 18 歳未満の多くの人に知られている.

62 Holmes は Lestrade 警部に事件はまだ解決していないと伝えた.

63 Nick は物事を分析するのは苦手だが, すばらしい創造性を発揮する.

64 車はよい交通手段だが, 環境を害する.

65 思っていたより緊張した.

66 Lori は私たちに彼女の知られたくないやばい秘密を話してくれた. その秘密は私たちを震え上がらせた.

67 そのチームにはトーナメントに出場するのに十分な人数のメンバーがいない.

68 日本企業でも, 責任ある地位につく女性がどんどん増えてきている.

69 Tsuchiya さんは大学生に IELTS のための試験対策を教えている.

70 彼氏はフランス料理の店に食事に連れて行ってくれると約束した.

---

67. enough もの・こと to do... 「……するのに十分なもの・こと」　68. = The number of women who have positions of responsibility is increasing.　69. give/teach 人 もの・こと = give/teach もの・こと to 人は中学で習う項目だが使いこなせる人は少ない.　70. = My boyfriend promised me that he would take me to dinner at a French restaurant.

71. The town hit by last month's big typhoon seems to lack vigor.

72. The problem is that we still don't know much about the virus.

73. People are afraid that the Prime Minister will make another big mistake.

74. When I was in high school, I was on the basketball team.

75. The speaker looked annoyed when one lady asked him too many questions.

76. Conrad does not trust people who use fake names on social media.

77. Nobody cares about whether Mr. Sawada used to be a famous musician.

78. In soccer, players kick a ball to move it toward their opponent's goal.

79. The teacher asked his students to be quiet, but they just kept talking.

80. Many of us found it difficult to study for Ms. Harlow's math class.

---

71. lack vigor「活気がなくなる」は覚えておきたいコロケーション． 72. The problem/fact/truth is that ~
「問題／事実／真実は~ということである」． = The problem is that we don't know much about the virus
yet． 73. be afraid/certain/angry/... that ~「~ということを恐れている／確信している／怒っている／……」．
74. ▲When I was a high school student, I belonged to the basketball club. は間違いではないがやや不
自然． 75. = When one lady asked the speaker too many questions, he looked annoyed. SV¹ 接続詞

71 先月の大きな台風の被害を受けたその町は活気を失っているように思える.

72 問題は，私たちがそのウイルスについてまだよく知らないということだ.

73 人々は総理大臣がまた大きな過ちを犯しはしないだろうかと恐れている.

74 高校の時，バスケ部に入っていた.

75 1人の女性があまりにたくさんの質問をした時，講演者は不快そうだった.

76 Conrad は SNS で偽名を使う人間を信用しない.

77 Sawada さんがかつて有名な音楽家だったかどうかは誰も気にかけない.

78 サッカーは敵のゴールに向かってボールを蹴るスポーツだ.

79 その先生は生徒たちに静かにするように言ったが，彼らは話すのをやめなかった.

80 私たちの多くは，Harlow 先生の数学のクラスで勉強していくのは難しいと気づいた.

SV². = 接続詞 SV², SV¹. 76. people who use fake names on social media 77. ✗ Everybody doesn't care... . 78. ボールを蹴るのはサッカーではなく選手なので，✗ Soccer kicks a ball… としないこと. 79. ask/tell/order 人 to *do* 「人に……するように頼む／言う／命令する」. 80. find もの・こと 状態 「もの・ことが状態とわかる」の応用. find it 状態 to *do*... 「……するのは状態とわかる」.

81 Many scientists consider this book to be the most authoritative on the topic.

82 I learned from three years in the school orchestra that effort pays off.

83 It is dangerous to make a big change in a system without careful consideration.

84 Before marrying her husband, Sarah was working at a bakery in Kansas City.

85 Many young people left the town because they could not find jobs there.

86 Gayla showed us her German car, which she bought from her best friend.

87 The coach gave us very clear directions so that all of us could understand.

88 Donald Trump, who used to be a reality show host, became a US president.

89 Eric was very good-looking and nice to everybody, so most girls in class liked him.

90 Some people think Japan should have more immigrants, while other people are against the idea.

---

81. This book is considered to be the most authoritative on the topic. のように受け身で使われることも多い. 82. = Three years in the school orchestra taught me that effort pays off. learn from 体験 that 教訓「体験から教訓を学んだ」, 体験 teach 人 教訓「体験は人に教訓を教えてくれる」. 83. a big change in a system without careful consideration で長い名詞のカタマリ.

81 多くの科学者はこの本がこの話題に関して最も信頼できるものだと考えている.

82 私は吹奏楽部に所属した 3 年間で努力は報われるということを学んだ.

83 よく考えずにシステムに大きな変更をするのは危険だ.

84 現在の夫と結婚する前は, Sarah はカンザスシティーのパン屋で働いていた.

85 仕事が見つからないので, 多くの若者はその町を後にした.

86 Gayla は私たちに彼女のドイツ車を見せてくれたが, その車は親友から買ったものだった.

87 監督は私たちみんなが理解できるようにとても明確な指示を出した.

88 Donald Trump 氏, かつてはリアリティー番組の司会者だったのだが, アメリカ大統領になった.

89 Eric は容姿がよく, 誰にでも親切なので, クラスのほとんどの女子は彼のことが好きだった.

90 日本はもっと移民を受け入れた方がよいという人がいる一方, その考えに反対する人もいる.

---

84. = Before she married her husband, ...　85. 結果 because 原因　86. , which「そしてそれは」補足情報
87. so that 目的「目的ということになるように」.　88. ..., who「そしてその人は」補足情報　89. 原因, so 結果
90. 通常は, SV¹, while SV².「SV¹ である一方 SV²」 While SV¹, SV².「SV¹ だが, SV²」

91 Mr. Queen's job was to interview the large number of people who knew the victim.

92 What everybody wants to know is how the director gets ideas for her movies.

93 We all wanted to know what had happened between Sally and Matt on that day.

94 A couple of people saw Amanda and Gary having a big argument in the Indian restaurant.

95 Mr. Marlow has to choose between spending time with his family and leading a big project.

96 College students ought to gain work experience as long as they make enough time to study.

97 Practice during the camp was so tough that a lot of members thought about leaving the team.

98 If the police had listened to the girl, she would not have been attacked by her stalker.

99 If I were the leader of this country, I would do whatever I could to grow the economy.

100 Billie Eilish, who a lot of people in her generation admire, performed in front of a big audience.

---

91. the large number of people <u>who knew the victim</u> 92. how SV「どのように S が……する／であるのか」
93. what does/is「何が……する／であるのか」 94. see 人 *doing* は行動の途中経過を見るというニュアンスがある.（→ 36）95. 動詞 choose と名詞 choice の混用をする学習者が多い. 96. 主張 as long as 条件.
97. so 状態 that 結果「あまりに状態なので結果」.

91 Queen 氏の仕事は被害者を知るたくさんの人々に聞き込みをすることだった.

92 みんなが知りたいことは，その監督は映画のアイディアをどのようにして見つけるのかということだ.

93 その日 Sally と Matt の間に何が起きたのか，私たちみんなが知りたかった.

94 Amanda と Gary がそのインド料理店内で激しい言い争いをしているのを数人の人が目撃している.

95 Marlow さんは家族との時間を過ごすか，大きなプロジェクトを率いるか，どちらかを選択しなくてはいけない.

96 勉強する時間が十分に取れる限り，大学生は就労体験を積むべきだ.

97 合宿中の練習があまりにきつかったので，多くの部員は退部を考えた.

98 もし，警察がその女の子の言うことに耳を傾けていれば，彼女がストーカーに襲われることもなかっただろう.

99 私がこの国の指導者なら，経済発展のためにできることは何だってやる.

100 Billie Eilish は同世代の多くの人々のあこがれだが，その彼女が大観衆の前でパフォーマンスを見せた.

---

98. 過去のことに関する仮定は，If S had -ed/en, S would have -ed/en. 　99. 現実にありえない仮定は If S 過去形, S would/could/... do. ただの条件を述べるときは，If S 現在形, S will/can/should/... do.：If you want to learn about music, you should ask Chris. 　100. ..., who「そしてその人は」補足情報. S who V (→ 88) だけでなく，S¹ who S²V も使える.

Chapter 2

センテンスを
つなげる

ここでは，最初のセンテンスから次のセンテンスへ
とどのように展開していくのかを学びましょう．論
理・構成面の土台となる，テキストに「つながり」を
出すスキルを学びます．

センテンスに別のセンテンスをつなげて展開する

Chapter 1 では，自分の言いたいことを簡潔なセンテンスで表現することを学びました．Chapter 2 では，これを土台に，センテンスの後ろに，それにつながる新たなセンテンスを置くことでテキストを展開していく方法を学びます．

　文章を展開する際に意識しなければいけないことは，センテンス間に cohesion（つながり＝前後に書かれていることが形式的・内容的にも無理なくつながっていること）があることです．では，どのようにして cohesion を出すのかというと，イギリスの言語学者 Michael Halliday による以下のモデルが広く知られています．

1. **Reference words** 指示語の使用

Few people came to Joe's art exhibition. **This** disappointed him. 指示語

Joe の絵画展にはほとんど人が来なかった．**このこと**は彼をがっかりさせた．

2. **Repeated words/ideas** 語・内容の繰り返し

Eric's hobby is performing **magic** tricks. Doing **magic** gives him extra money. 語の繰り返し

Eric の趣味は**マジック**のネタの披露です．**マジック**をすることで臨時収入を得ています．

3. **Transition markers** つなぎ言葉の使用

Male students loosen their ties, untuck their shirts, or wear their pants below the waistline. **Similarly**, female students hitch their skirts way above their knees. つなぎ語

男子生徒はネクタイをゆるめ，シャツの裾を出したり，腰よりも下げてズボンをはいたりします．**同じように**，女子生徒は膝よりもずっと高い位置までスカートの裾を上げます．

4. Substitution 〈代用語の使用〉

I was not ready to accept the offer at that time. I should **have done it (= have accepted the offer)**, though.

代用語

そのときは，その提案を受け入れる準備ができていなかった．**そうする**（＝受け入れる）べきだったのだが．

5. Ellipsis 〈語・表現の省略〉

One problem is that we don't have enough money. Another **(problem)** is that we are short on time.

省略

問題の一つは十分なお金がないことだ．**他には**（＝他の**問題**としては）時間が足りないということがある．

6. Topic development 〈トピックの展開〉

　この中で一番大事なのは 6. **Topic development**（トピックの展開）で，Section 1 から Section 3 を使って，英語の論理の原理・原則（**抽象から具体へ**（abstract to concrete）、**一般から特定へ**（general to specific）、**知っていることから知らないことへ**（known to new））を知り，トピックを自然に展開するスキルを学びます．Section 4 から Section 15 は展開パターンごとの 3. **Transition markers**（つなぎ言葉）をどう使うかが強調されていますが，cohesion を生み出す 1.～ 6. のすべてのスキルが練習できるようになっています．

　論理の原理・原則と展開パターンに馴染んでいないと，いくら文法や単語が得意でもなかなかライティングができません．しかし，ここに注意を向ける学習者や指導者は少ないようです．本書はここに焦点を思いきって当てたので．この機会にぜひ論理の原理・原則と代表的な展開パターンを身につけましょう．

　センテンスに別のセンテンスをつなげるスキルを学ぶ Chapter 2 は本書の心臓部です．本書の使い方（p. 7）に示したように，必ず Exercise は自分なりの解答を作り，のちに Sample Answers と比べるという作業を行なってください．頭と手を使って作業をしないと，論理の原則・展開のスキルはなかなか自分のものにはならないからです．この段階では文法の正確さや表現の洗練度は副次的なものと考えてください．気になる人はネイティヴの知人や AI に添削してもらっても良いですが，論理・構成面で不安がなくなれば，インプットに比例して少しずつ洗練された文構造・表現が使えるようになってきます．

Chapter 1　センテンスを組み立てる

Chapter 2　センテンスをつなげる

Chapter 3　文章をまとめる

Abstract to concrete

抽象から具体へ

> 英語の論理では抽象的な (abstract: ざっくり・ふんわりとした具体性のない概念的な) ことを先に述べ, 具体的な (concrete: 概念や推測ではなく実体のあるものに基づく) ことを後に続けるのが原則です.

Examples

　ここでは 2 つのセンテンスを「抽象 → 具体」と並べる練習をします. 最初は例を確認します.「抽象 → 具体」の流れが, 読み手の知りたい順番に情報を流していることをつかみましょう.

1. Raccoon dogs really look like raccoons. They have long, soft, brown fur around their bodies and masks of black fur around their eyes.

   タヌキはアライグマによく似ている. 長くて柔らかい茶色の毛が体を覆っていて, 目の周りの毛は黒くマスクのようになっている.

   ■ アライグマに似ている (抽象) → 似ていることを示す描写 (具体)

   ► Look like raccoons. → How? という読み手の期待に応えて文章展開していると考えましょう.

2. The female judo player is very strong. She is said to have fought against a bear and won.

   その女性の柔道選手はとても強い. 彼女は熊と戦って勝ったといわれている.

   ■ 強い (抽象) → 熊を打ち負かした (具体)

3. Aaron is very smart. He knows a lot of things and can always find solutions to problems very quickly.

Aaron はとても頭が良い. 彼は物知りで, いつもすぐに問題の解決策を見つけられる.
■ 頭が良い（抽象）→ 物知りで問題解決が早い（具体）

4. Kimberly is very kind. She always offers help to people in need.

Kimberly はとても親切だ. 彼女はいつも必要な人に手を差し伸べる.
■ 親切（抽象）→ 人助けする（具体）

5. Tastes differ. My friend Mika likes boys who are good at sports, but I like intelligent ones.

人の好みはさまざまだ. 友達の Mika はスポーツが得意な男の子が好きだが, 私は頭が良い男の子が好きだ.
■ 好みはさまざま（抽象）→ Mika と私の男の子の好み（具体）

6. Kevin loves to be close to nature. He left his job to live in a small town surrounded by mountains.

Kevin は自然の近くにいるのが好きだ. 彼は山に囲まれた小さな町に住むために仕事を辞めた.
■ 自然が好き（抽象）→ 田舎への移住（具体）

7. Emiko is a hard worker. She teaches in three universities, does research, and looks after three kids and her parents.

Emiko は働き者だ. 彼女は 3 つの大学で教えていて, 研究もして, さらには 3 人の子どもと両親の面倒を見ている.
■ 働き者（抽象）→ 3 つの大学での勤務＋研究＋3 人の子育て（具体）

8. Jason seems to know a lot of things. He can speak on topics from wrestling and fashion trends to the stock market.

Jason はたくさんのことを知っているようだ. 彼はレスリングから流行りのファッション, 株式市場まで話すことができる.
■ 物知り（抽象）→ レスリング・ファッション・株（具体）

9. Erica hates technology. She still subscribes to print newspapers, and she never texts or emails.

Erica はテクノロジーが嫌いだ. 彼女はいまだに紙の新聞を購読し, チャットや E メールはやらない.
■ テクノロジー嫌い（抽象）→ 紙の新聞＋チャット・メールはやらない（具体）

10. The US government decided to withdraw from the battlefield. More than 30,000 soldiers are leaving Afghanistan and returning home.

アメリカ政府は戦場から撤退することを決めた. 30,000 人以上の兵士がアフガニスタンを出て, 帰国する.
■ 戦場からの撤退（抽象）→ アフガニスタンからの兵士の帰国（具体）

1-10 の各々が論理的に（「抽象→具体」の流れで）つながるように，空所を埋めてみましょう．必ず自分なりの解答を作ってみてください．

1 Darin is very tall. _____.

2 Mark is very athletic. _____
_____.

3 Shawn is talkative. _____
_____.

4 Andrew is very fashionable. _____
_____.

5 Honesty pays. _____
_____.

6 Patrick made a big decision. _____
_____.

7 Keiko has a good reputation in the workplace. _____
_____.

8 Laura has gained weight. _____
_____.

9 More and more kids go to college. _____
_____
_____.

10 The truth comes out. _____
_____.

完成したら，自分の書いたものと次ページの Sample Answers をよく比べてみましょう．

Sample Answers

❶ Darin is very tall. <u>His height is over 190 centimeters.</u>

Darin はとても背が高い. 彼の身長は 190 センチ以上ある.

別解 Darin is very tall. <u>He is taller than any other student in class.</u>

Darin はとても背が高い. 彼はクラスの誰よりも背が高い.

❷ Mark is very athletic. <u>He runs more than 10 kilometers, bikes 30 kilometers, and swims one kilometer every single day.</u>

Mark はすごいスポーツマンだ. 彼は毎日 10 キロ以上走り, 30 キロ自転車に乗り, 1 キロ泳ぐ.

別解 Mark is very athletic. <u>He exercises regularly and is very muscular.</u>

Mark はすごいスポーツマンだ. 彼は日頃から運動していて筋肉質だ.

❸ Shawn is talkative. <u>Once he starts speaking, you can't stop him.</u>

Shawn はよくしゃべる. しゃべり出すと止まらない.

別解 Shawn is talkative. <u>He talks to everybody and can hold a conversation for a long time.</u>

Shawn はよくしゃべる. 彼は誰にでも話しかけて, 会話を長い時間続けることができる.

❹ Andrew is very fashionable. <u>He wears clothes in a very unique manner.</u>

Andrew はとてもおしゃれである. 彼の服の着こなしはたいへん個性的だ.

別解 Andrew is very fashionable. <u>He wears fancy clothes from head to toe.</u>

Andrew はとてもおしゃれである. 彼は目立つ服を頭のてっぺんから爪先まで身につけている.

Chapter 1

センテンスを組み立てる

Chapter 2

センテンスをつなげる

Chapter 3

文章をまとめる

❺ Honesty pays. I never hide any of my mistakes, so my boss trusts me.

正直者は報われる. 私は決して自分のどんな誤ちも隠さないので, 上司はそんな私を信頼している.

別解 Honesty pays. I found a 10,000 yen bill at a café, told a waitress about it, and later on the girl and I somehow started dating.

正直者は報われる. 喫茶店で一万円札を拾って, ウェイトレスに教えたら, のちにどういうわけかその子とつきあうようになった.

❻ Patrick made a big decision. He left a large consulting firm to start his own business.

Patrick は大きな決断をした. 彼は自分の事業を立ち上げるために, 大きなコンサルタント会社を辞めた.

別解 Patrick made a big decision. He stopped eating carbs to lose weight.

Patrick は大きな決断をした. 彼はやせるために炭水化物を食べるのをやめた.

❼ Keiko has a good reputation in the workplace. None of her colleagues say bad things about her.

Keiko は職場で評判が良い. 同僚の中に彼女の悪口を言う人はひとりもいない.

別解 Keiko has a good reputation in the workplace. Everybody thinks that she works hard and communicates well.

Keiko は職場で評判が良い. だれもがよく働き, 気にかけてくれると考えている.

❽ Laura has gained weight. Last year, she was 54 kilograms, but she is over 60 kilograms now.

Laura は体重が増えた. 去年 54 キロだったのだが, 今は 60 キロを超えている.

別解 Laura has gained weight. She started living alone and has probably changed her diet in a bad way.

Laura は体重が増えた. 彼女は一人暮らしを始めて, たぶんよくない食習慣を身につけてしまったのだ.

9 More and more kids go to college. In the past, less than 30% of high school graduates entered colleges or universities, but now about half of them do.

大学に進学する子どもが増えている. 過去には高校卒業者で短大や大学に進むのは 30 パーセント以下だったが, 今では半分ぐらいになっている.

別解 More and more kids go to college. In the past, college graduates were considered to be elites, but not anymore.

大学に進学する子どもが増えている. 過去には大学生はエリートと考えられていたが, いまはもうそうではない.

10 The truth comes out. All the lies Donald told were eventually detected and exposed.

真実はいずれ明るみに出る. Donald がついた多くの嘘は最終的に見破られて, 暴かれた.

別解 The truth comes out. The handsome man told many young women that he owned a big IT company, but it turned out to be a fraud.

真実はいずれ明るみに出る. そのイケメン男性は多くの若い女性に大きな IT 会社のオーナーだといっていたが, 詐欺であることがわかった.

General to specific

一般から特定へ

英語の論理としては，一般的な（general: 広く，多くの人にかかわる）ことを先に，特定の（specific: 個別，固有に関する）ことは後に述べるのが原則です．

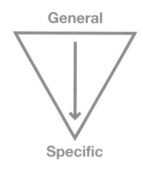

General

Specific

Examples

1. Many Japanese girls try what they dreamt of doing but couldn't after graduating from high school. For example, Sayaka dyed her hair pink.

   多くの日本人の女の子は高校を卒業後，やりたかったのにできなかったことをやる．例えば Sayaka は髪をピンクに染めた．

   ■ 多くの日本人の女の子（一般）→ Sayaka（特定）／やりたかったことをやる（一般）→ 髪をピンクに染める（特定）

2. Health is something that everybody is concerned about. For people over 60, it is probably their biggest concern.

   健康はみんなが関心を抱いていることだ．60 歳以上の人にとってはおそらく最大の関心事だ．

   ■ みんな（一般）→ 60 歳以上の人（特定）

3. A lot of big earthquakes hit Japan. The one that occurred in East Japan in 2011 had a severe impact on the whole country.

   多くの大地震が日本を襲った．2011 年に東日本で起こったものは国全体に深刻な衝撃を与えた．

   ■ 大地震（一般）→ 東日本大震災（特定）

4. Everybody has a secret. Especially, teenagers often have something that they don't want to share with their parents or other adults.

誰もが秘密を抱えている. とりわけ, 10代は親や他の大人には言えないような秘密を抱えていることが多い.
■ みんな (一般) → 10代 (特定)

5. Moving house is one of the most important events in our lives. I moved to Osaka at the age of 12, and this has been the biggest change in my life.

引っ越しは, 人生の中で最も重要な出来事のひとつである. 私は12歳のとき大阪に引っ越して, これがこれまでのところ人生最大の変化だ.
■ 引っ越し (一般) → 12歳のときの自分の引っ越し (特定)

6. A job will often change our lives. My life changed a lot when I got my first job at a coffee shop.

仕事は私たちの人生を変えることがよくある. 喫茶店で初めて仕事を見つけた時, 私の人生は大きく変わった.
■ 仕事 (一般) → 自分の最初の仕事 (特定)

7. Eating less and exercising more will help you lose weight. My sister started running five kilometers in the morning and stopped eating dinner, and she lost 15 kilograms in three months.

食べる量を減らして運動を増やすと体重を減らせる. 私の妹は朝5キロ走り始め夕食をカットしたら, 3ヶ月で15キロ痩せた.
■ 食事制限 (一般) → 夕食を抜く (特定) ／運動 (一般) → 5キロ走る (特定) ／減量 (一般) → 15キロの減量 (特定)

8. Many adults in Japan also hold part-time work. My father works part-time at a gasoline station.

日本では多くの成人がアルバイトもしている. 私の父はガソリンスタンドでアルバイトしている.
■ 多くの成人 (一般) → 私の父 (特定) ／アルバイト (一般) → ガソリンスタンドでの仕事 (特定)

9. Danny and William are quite alike. In particular, they communicate with other people in almost the same way.

DannyとWilliamはそっくりだ. 特に, 他の人へのコミュニケーションの取り方はほとんど同じだ.
■ 似ている (一般) → コミュニケーションの取り方が同じ (特定)

10. It is totally wrong to steal someone else's idea. Students who submit other people's work as their own will be severely punished.

人の考えを盗むのは完全に間違っている. 他人がやったものを自分がやったものとして提出する学生は厳しく罰せられる.
■ 剽窃・盗作 (一般) → 他人の課題を自分のものとして提出 (特定)

Exercise

1-10 の各々が論理的に（「一般→特定」の流れで）つながるように，空所を埋めてみましょう．必ず自分なりの解答を作ってみてください．

1 Most people have the experience of playing a sport in school. When I was in [   ], I [   ] [   ].

2 There are a lot of ways to send messages to other people. In particular, [   ] is one of the most common methods.

3 Some people become wild in summer. [   ] [   ].

4 Everybody has a chance to make their dream come true. [   ] [   ].

5 Working as a volunteer can help you learn what is not taught at school. [   ] [   ].

6 Having a hobby makes your life enjoyable. [   ] [   ] [   ].

7 A gambling addiction is dangerous. [   ] [   ].

8 People naturally compare themselves with others. [   ] [   ] [   ].

9 Each community has different customs and conventions.

	.

10 When tired, people make stupid mistakes.

	.

完成したら，自分の書いたものと次の Sample Answers をよく比べてみましょう.

─(Sample Answers)─────────────────

1 Most people have the experience of playing a sport in school. When I was in <u>high school</u>, I <u>was on the basketball team</u>.

多くの人は学校でスポーツをした経験がある. 高校の時，私はバスケットボール部だった.

別解 Most people have the experience of playing a sport in school. When I was in <u>college</u>, I <u>swam after school almost every day</u>.

多くの人は学校でスポーツをした経験がある. 大学生のとき, 私はほとんど毎日放課後に水泳をしていた.

2 There are a lot of ways to send messages to other people. In particular, <u>texting</u> is one of the most common methods.

他の人に連絡する手段はたくさんある. テキストメッセージはとりわけ最もよく用いられる方法のひとつだ.

別解 There are a lot of ways to send messages to other people. In particular, <u>using social media</u> is one of the most common methods.

他の人に連絡する手段はたくさんある. SNS はとりわけ最もよく使われる方法のひとつだ.

3 Some people become wild in summer. <u>My younger sister went to the beach, got to know some surfers, and had relationships with a few of them</u>.

夏になると大胆な行動をとる人もいる. 妹は海に行って，サーファーと知り合いになった. その中の何人かと深い仲になった.

別解 Some people become wild in summer. <u>Jim and Todd traveled across the country and a lot of crazy things happened in each place they visited</u>.

夏になると大胆な行動をとる人もいる. Jim と Todd は国内を旅行したときに，旅先ではたくさんの信じられない騒動が起きた.

❹ Everybody has a chance to make their dream come true. <u>For Sarah, it came last year—she passed an audition for the leading role in a movie.</u>

誰もが自分の夢をかなえる機会がある. Sarah にとっては去年がそうだった. 彼女は映画の主役のオーディションに受かった.

別解 Everybody has a chance to make their dream come true. <u>As a kid, Bill wanted to be a company president, so he started his own business after he graduated from college.</u>

誰もが自分の夢をかなえる機会がある. 子供の頃, Bill は社長になりたかった, それで大学を卒業後, 自分で事業を始めた.

❺ Working as a volunteer can help you learn what is not taught at school. <u>I volunteered for a political campaign and learned our country's political system firsthand.</u>

ボランティア活動をすると学校では教わらないことを学ぶ機会がある. 私は政治キャンペーンのボランティアをして, この国の政治システムを直に学んだ.

別解 Working as a volunteer can help you learn what is not taught at school. <u>I volunteered in an area hit by a natural disaster and learned how hard the lives of those living in the damaged area were.</u>

ボランティア活動をすると学校では教わらないことを学ぶ機会がある. 私は自然災害の被害を受けた地域でボランティア活動をして, 被災地域の生活がどんなものであるかを学んだ.

❻ Having a hobby makes your life enjoyable. <u>For Steve Paydon, riding a motorcycle is an indispensable hobby.</u>

趣味を持つことは人生をより楽しいものにする. Steve Paydon にとってはバイクに乗ることがかけがえのない趣味だ.

別解 Having a hobby makes your life enjoyable. <u>Eric Berg started shooting videos as a hobby but now he can't live without it.</u>

趣味を持つことは人生をより楽しいものにする. Eric Berg は趣味として映像製作をはじめたが, 今はそれがなくては生きられなくなった.

❼ A gambling addiction is dangerous. <u>My dad was addicted to horse racing and spent a large amount of money on races.</u>

ギャンブル中毒は危険だ. 父は競馬中毒になり, たくさんのお金をレースに注ぎ込んだ.

別解 A gambling addiction is dangerous. <u>Conrad goes to a casino in Las Vegas every year and spends a lot of money.</u>

ギャンブル中毒は危険だ. Conrad はラスベガスのカジノに毎年行って, たくさんのお金を使ってしまう.

8 People naturally compare themselves with others. <u>When other kids perform better than them, they feel envy or unhappiness</u>.

人は自然と他人を自分と比べる. 他の子どもが自分よりもうまくやると，うらやんだり悲しくなったりする.

別解 People naturally compare themselves with others. <u>I am always concerned about what my sister does and try to do better than her</u>.

人は自然と他人を自分と比べる。私はいつも妹がすることが気になり，彼女よりも上を行こうとする.

9 Each community has different customs and conventions. <u>In Japan, people take off their shoes before entering a house, while many people in Western countries wear their shoes inside houses</u>.

それぞれのコミュニティーには異なる習慣や決まり事がある. 日本では，家に入るときに靴を脱ぐが，欧米諸国では家の中でも靴を履いている.

別解 Each community has different customs and conventions. <u>In France, people often kiss as a greeting, but in Japan doing so would embarrass people</u>.

それぞれのコミュニティーには異なる習慣や決まり事がある. フランスではあいさつにキスをするが，日本でそれをすると人々に恥ずかしい思いをさせてしまう.

10 When tired, people make stupid mistakes. <u>My sister was exhausted this morning and put salt instead of sugar in her coffee</u>.

疲れているとき，人はばかな間違いをする. 姉は今朝疲れていて，コーヒーに砂糖ではなく塩を入れた.

別解 When tired, people make stupid mistakes. <u>Laura attended yesterday's sales meeting with her pajamas on</u>.

疲れているとき，人はばかな間違いをする. Laura は昨日の営業会議に寝巻きで参加した.

Section 3

Known to new

知っていることから
知らないことへ

読み手にわかってもらうためには，情報が相手が理解しやすい順序で述べられて
いないといけません．複数のセンテンスを述べるとき，それぞれのセンテンスを
相手がすでに知っている（Known）要素で始めて，相手の知らない新しい（New）
情報につなげる．そして，次のセンテンスは New であったその情報を Known
として始める……，というように繰り返していくのが原則です．

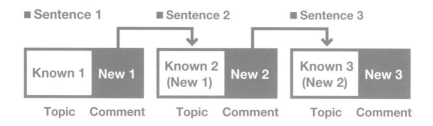

Tips to Check 前出の要素を代名詞で受ける

Yesterday, I saw a very strange boy on the train. He was wearing a pink sweatshirt and red pants.

昨日私は，電車で奇妙な少年を見た．彼はピンクのトレーナーと赤いズボンを着ていた．

➤ 最初のセンテンスでは a very strange boy on the train という New information かつトピックで終わり，
これを受ける He を次のセンテンスの Known information として始めています．トピックを引き継いで，
つながり感を出すためです．その後，a pink sweatshirt and red pants とトピックの人物の服装，New
information で終わらせています．

Let's Practice!

There are a few good books about digital currencies. [   ] will help you understand what cryptocurrencies, such as Bitcoin, are.

仮想通貨について何冊か良い本がある. これらの本はビットコインなどの仮想通貨についてあなたが理解を深めるのを助けるだろう.

> ► 解答：**They**　There is/are ... の後がセンテンスのトピック＝ New information です. これを they で受け, Known information として続くセンテンスを展開しています.

....

Inside the room, there was a cat. [   ] was black and making high-pitched sounds.

その部屋には猫がいた. 黒い猫で, 高い声で鳴いていた.

> ► 解答：**It**　中学校 1 年で習う There was a cat inside the room. という語順になっていないのは, (inside) the room が Known information で, New information である a cat により焦点を当てたいからです.

Tips to Check　前出の要素を代名詞や他の言葉に置き換える①

Paul waited for his girlfriend at the cafe for more than three hours, but she didn't come. This made him angry.

Paul は彼女を喫茶店で 3 時間以上も待ったが, 現われなかった. それで彼は怒った.

> ► 第 2 センテンスの this は第 1 センテンスの内容すべてを受けています.

Sally's husband left her for her best friend. This experience made her distrustful of people.

Sally の夫は彼女を捨てて彼女の親友の元に行った. この体験が彼女を人間不信にした.

> ► 第 1 センテンスの内容を〈this ＋名詞〉でまとめています.

Let's Practice!

Five years ago, I had a great job and a great girlfriend. [   ] was the best moment of my life.

5 年前, 良い仕事に就いていて, すてきな彼女がいた. それが人生の最高点だった.

> ► 解答：**That**　第 2 センテンスの that は, 第 1 センテンスの内容すべてを受けています.

....

Matt hurt his left leg while playing soccer. [   ] [   ] forced him to stop exercising and study a lot.

Matt はサッカーをしているときに左足に負傷した. この負傷で運動を控えてたくさん勉強する羽目になった.

> ► 解答：**This injury**　hurt his left leg while playing soccer → this injury と言い換え.

John Watson first met Sherlock Holmes on January 1, 1881. This encounter drastically changed the two gentlemen's lives.

1881 年の元旦に John Watson は初めて Sherlock Holmes に出会った. この出会いが劇的にふたりの人生を変えた.

- first met という動詞のカタマリを〈this ＋名詞〉で言い換えるときに encounter というやや高級な語を使うことでよりつながりが生まれています.

Let's Practice!

Conrad is handsome. ☐ ☐ attracts the attention of women around him.

Conrad はハンサムだ. 彼の容貌は周りの女性の注意を惹く.

- **解答：His appearance** トピック = Conrad, コメント = (is) handsome という第 1 センテンスの内容を, his という所有限定詞と appearance という名詞でまとめてつながりを出しています.

....

Sherlock told Ms. Woods that he could solve the case by the next day. ☐ ☐ totally surprised me.

Sherlock は Woods 夫人に翌日までに事件を解決してみせると言った. こう断言したことは私を本当に驚かせた.

- **解答：This declaration** this declaration の内容は that 以下です.

Rich likes to help people. Helping others gives him energy.

Rich は人助けが好きだ. 他人を助けることで彼は自分に力が湧くのを感じる.

- 第 2 センテンスの Known information を動詞の doing 形で始める方法もあります. 第 1 センテンスの New information である to help people をそっくりそのまま使うのではなく, people を others に言い換えています. to do は主語には通常しない（→ Chapter 1 ▨）こともあり, doing 形が使われています.

Exercise

1-11 の各々が論理的に（「知っていること→知らないこと」の流れで）つながるように，空所を埋めてみましょう．必ず自分なりの解答を作ってみてください．

1 Last summer, I met a _____. He/She was _____
_____.

2 There are some good instruction videos on online
conferencing. They _____
_____.

3 At the end of the street, there was a _____ man.
He _____
_____.

4 Andrew is extremely smart. His cleverness _____
_____.

5 Few people came to Joe's art exhibition. This
_____ him.

6 Three years ago, my best friend deceived me, I lost my
job, and my wife left me. That was _____.

7 Tom bumped his car into another car. _____
made him drive more carefully afterwards.

8 Sue _____.
This success gave her a lot of confidence.

9 Mr. Young _____.
This sad event changed his character.

10 Kelly's boss guaranteed that she would get a position
with more responsibility. This promise _____.

11 Eric's hobby is performing magic tricks. ⬚⬚⬚⬚⬚⬚
gives him extra money.

完成したら，自分の書いたものと次の Sample Answers をよく比べてみましょう．

┌─ Sample Answers ┐

❶ Last summer, I met a girl. She was exceptionally pretty.

去年の夏，私はひとりの女の子に会った．彼女はたぐいまれな美しさだった．

別解 Last summer, I met a movie director. He was extremely creative.

去年の夏，私は映画監督に出会った．彼はものすごく創造性がある人だった．

❷ There are some good instruction videos on online conferencing. They will help you learn how to hold online meetings.

オンライン会議のやり方を教える動画はたくさんある．これらの動画はオンライン会議の開き方を学ぶのに役立つ．

別解 There are some good instruction videos on online conferencing. They are available on the internet for free.

オンライン会議のやり方を教える動画はたくさんある．これらの動画はインターネット上で無料で入手できる．

❸ At the end of the street, there was a tall, thin man. He was looking at me accusingly.

その通りの突き当たりには，背の高いやせた男が立っていた．彼は私を責めるように見つめていた．

別解 At the end of the street, there was a wounded man. He was lying on the ground.

その通りの突き当たりには，けがをした男がいた．彼は地面に横になっていた．

❹ Andrew is extremely smart. His cleverness is way ahead of other people's.

Andrew はものすごく頭が良い．彼の頭の良さは他の人たちを凌駕している．

別解 Andrew is extremely smart. His cleverness is not recognized by many people, though.

Andrew はものすごく頭が良いのに，（彼の頭の良さは）多くの人には認識されていない．

5 Few people came to Joe's art exhibition. This <u>disappointed</u> him.

Joe の絵画展にはほとんど人が来なかった．（このことで）彼はがっかりした．

別解 Few people came to Joe's art exhibition. This <u>shocked</u> him.

Joe の絵画展にはほとんど人が来なかった．（このことで）彼はショックを受けた．

6 Three years ago, my best friend deceived me, I lost my job, and my wife left me. That was <u>a nightmare</u>.

3 年前，親友に騙されて，失職し，妻には逃げられた．（それは）悪夢だった．

別解 Three years ago, my best friend deceived me, I lost my job, and my wife left me. That was <u>a disaster</u>.

3 年前，親友に騙されて，失職し，妻には逃げられた．（それは）災難だった．

7 Tom bumped his car into another car. <u>This accident</u> made him drive more carefully afterwards.

Tom は他の車に自分の車をぶつけた．この事故の後，彼は安全運転をするようになった．

別解 Tom bumped his car into another car. <u>This experience</u> made him drive more carefully afterwards.

Tom は他の車に自分の車をぶつけた．この経験から彼は安全運転をするようになった．

8 Sue <u>studied hard and passed a very difficult entrance exam</u>. This success gave her a lot of confidence.

Sue は一生懸命勉強して，大変難しい入試を突破した．この成功体験が彼女に大きな自信を与えた．

別解 Sue <u>went to an audition for a bit role but was offered a starring role</u>. This success gave her a lot of confidence.

Sue は端役のオーディションに行ったら，主役のオファーを受けた．この成功体験が彼女に大きな自信を与えた．

9 Mr. Young <u>lost his wife and son in an airplane accident</u>. This sad event changed his character.

Young 氏は妻と子どもを飛行機事故で失った．この悲しい出来事で彼の性格は変わってしまった．

別解 Mr. Young <u>was betrayed by his best friend and girlfriend</u>. This sad event changed his character.

Young 氏は親友と彼女に裏切られた．この悲しい出来事で彼の性格は変わってしまった．

⑩ Kelly's boss guaranteed that she would get a position with more responsibility. This promise <u>motivated her</u>.

Kelly の上司は彼女をもっと責任ある地位に就かせると保証した．この約束は彼女をやる気にさせた．

別解 Kelly's boss guaranteed that she would get a more responsible position. This promise <u>made her happy</u>.

Kelly の上司は彼女をもっと責任ある地位に就かせると保証した．この約束で彼女はうれしくなった．

⑪ Eric's hobby is performing magic tricks. <u>Doing magic</u> gives him extra money.

Eric の趣味はマジックを披露することだ．マジックをすることで彼は副収入を得ている．

別解 Eric's hobby is performing magic tricks. <u>It</u> gives him extra money.

（訳は上の解答に同じ）

Chapter 1　センテンスを組み立てる

Chapter 2　センテンスをつなげる

Chapter 3　文章をまとめる

To list ideas

列挙する

> 「列挙する」を英語では list という動詞を使いますが, リストを作るように, 2つ以上の考え, 事実, 理由を並べる表現方法です. まず何かを述べた後で「それにこれも」とどんどん追加していくのが基本です.

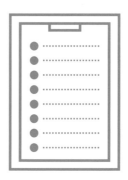

Common expressions

▸ also

▸ in addition

▸ additionally

▸ besides

▸ moreover

▸ first, … second, … third, …

▸ another

Tips to Check 列挙によく使われる and, also

列挙のためのつなぎというと and を思い浮かべるかもしれませんが, and は書き言葉ではセンテンスの中で語句をつなぐのに使い, センテンスとセンテンスをつなぐ際は避けるのが適切です.

Brenda stood up and walked out of the meeting room.

Brenda は立ち上がって会議室を後にした.

Installing solar panels on your house's roof is eco-friendly. **Also**, it will save electricity.

自分の家の屋根に太陽光パネルを設置するのは環境に良い．それに，電気代の節約になる．

■ 太陽光パネル設置の利点を列挙

➤ also は会話でも使われる最も普通の言葉です．上のように文頭に使われることもありますが，It also will ... のようにセンテンスの中で使うことも可能で，書き言葉においてはこちらが正しいとする保守的な人もいます．

Let's Practice! 解答は次ページ

Maria is good at sports, and ☐ ☐ a lot of things.

Maria はスポーツが得意な上に，いろいろなことを知っている．

A uniform is pretty expensive. In addition, they are ☐ ☐ ☐ wear for long hours.

制服はとてもお金がかかる．加えて，それらは，長時間着るのに着心地が良いものではない．

■ 制服の良くない点の列挙

A man broke into Sally's house. Additionally, ☐ ☐ her collection of watches.

ある男が Sally の家に忍び込んだ．さらに，時計のコレクションを盗んだ．

■ 男がした悪事の列挙

Rich wanted to help Danny out. Besides, the job ☐ ☐ .

Rich は Danny を手伝ってやりたかった．その上，その仕事は面白そうに思えた．

■ 仕事を引き受けた理由の列挙

Amy is good at playing guitar. Moreover, ☐ ☐ ☐ sing songs.

Amy はギターがうまい．それに，歌うのが好きだ．

■ 音楽関係の Amy の得意なこと，好きなことの列挙

➤ moreover は書き言葉用の硬めの表現です．furthermore とするとさらに物々しくなります．話し言葉では，スピーチなどを除いて，what's more となります．

列挙する前に，何について列挙するのか断り書きをすることもあります．

There are a few reasons you should not marry Mr. Robbins. First, you are too young to get married. Second, Mr. Robbins is not ready to get married either. Third, he probably doesn't love you.

Robbins さんと結婚しない方がいい理由はいくつかある．第1に，君は結婚するには若過ぎる．第2に Robbins さんも結婚する状況にはない．第3に，彼はたぶん君のことを好きじゃない．

■ 最初のセンテンスが示すように，結婚しない方がいい理由の列挙

Let's Practice!

In my opinion, people in the modern world lead better lives than those of fifty years ago. Firstly, the quality of education has remarkably improved over the past decades. ⬚⬚⬚ **that people have become more equal.**

私の考えでは，今の人々は50年前の人々よりも良い暮らしを送っていると思う．第1に，教育の質がここ数十年で目覚ましく良くなった．他の理由は，人々がより平等になったことだ．

■ 現在の人が過去の人よりも良い暮らしを送っていると考えられる理由の列挙

解答

she knows
not comfortable to
he stole
seemed interesting
she likes to
Another reason is

Exercise

1-7 の各々が論理的に（「列挙する」展開で）つながるように，空所を埋めてみましょう．必ず自分なりの解答を作ってみてください．

1 Taking a walk in your free time will help you relax. It also

_____.

2 Joan could not trust what Amanda said. In addition, ____

_____.

3 Taylor became popular because of her singing ability. Additionally, _____.

4 Conrad felt that it was not a smart idea to lend Mitch 4,000 yen. Besides, _____.

5 The middle-aged gentleman dyed his hair pink to impress his favorite female colleague. Moreover, _____

_____.

6 _____

_____. First, you have to know what you need to do to achieve your goal. Second, you have to make a schedule to work toward the goal. Third, you have to stick to the schedule until you accomplish your goal.

7 One problem is that we don't have enough money. Another

_____.

完成したら，自分の書いたものと次ページの Sample Answers をよく比べてみましょう．

❶ Taking a walk in your free time will help you relax. It **also** will keep you in good health.

時間があるときに散歩をすると気分がくつろぐ. 散歩は健康にも良い.

> **別解** Taking a walk in your free time will help you relax. It **also** will stop you from staying home and doing nothing.
>
> 時間があるときに散歩をすると気分がくつろぐ. それによって家で何もしないでいることがなくなる.

❷ Joan could not trust what Amanda said. **In addition**, she didn't like her personality.

Joan は Amanda の言うことが信じられなかった. それに, 彼女の性格も嫌いだった.

> **別解** Joan could not trust what Amanda said. **In addition**, she heard that Amanda often lied.
>
> Joan は Amanda の言うことが信じられなかった. それに, Amanda はよくうそをつくのだと聞いていた.

❸ Taylor became popular because of her singing ability. **Additionally**, her acting skills are well regarded.

Taylor は歌唱力で人気が出た. 加えて, 彼女の演技力も評価された.

> **別解** Taylor became popular because of her singing ability. **Additionally**, she knew how to get attention.
>
> Taylor は歌唱力で人気が出た. 加えて, 彼女は注目を集めるためにどう行動すればよいかがわかっていた.

❹ Conrad felt that it was not a smart idea to lend Mitch 4,000 yen. **Besides**, he only had 5,000 yen in his pocket.

Conrad は Mitch に 4,000 円も貸すのはよくないと思った. それに, ポケットには 5,000 円しかなかった.

> **別解** Conrad felt that it was not a smart idea to lend Mitch 4,000 yen. **Besides**, 4,000 yen was a lot of money for him then.
>
> Conrad は Mitch に 4,000 円も貸すのはよくないと思った. それに, 4000 円はそのときの彼にとっては大金だった.

5 The middle-aged gentleman dyed his hair pink to impress his favorite female colleague. **Moreover,** he bought a new sports car.

その中年男性は気に入った女性の同僚の気を惹こうと髪をピンク色に染めた．それだけでなく，新しいスポーツカーも買った．

別解 The middle-aged gentleman dyed his hair pink to impress his favorite female colleague. **Moreover,** he sent her a bouquet of red roses.

その中年男性は気に入った女性の同僚の気を惹こうと髪をピンク色に染めた．それだけでなく，彼は彼女に赤いバラの花束を贈った．

6 It is easy to achieve any goal if you do the following three things. **First,** you have to know what you need to do to achieve your goal. **Second,** you have to make a schedule to work toward the goal. **Third,** you have to stick to the schedule until you accomplish your goal.

以下の3つのことをすれば，どんな目標も達成するのはたやすい．第1に，目標を成し遂げるのに何が必要かを知ることだ．第2に，目標までのスケジュールを作らないといけない．第3に，目標達成までそのスケジュールを絶対に守ることだ．

別解 To realize your goal, you have to do these things. **First,** you have to know what you need to do to achieve your goal. **Second,** you have to make a schedule to work toward the goal. **Third,** you have to stick to the schedule until you accomplish your goal.

目標を実現するには以下のことをしないといけない．（以下，上の解答に同じ）

7 One problem is that we don't have enough money. **Another** is that we are short on time.

問題の1つは十分なお金がないことだ．もうひとつの問題は時間が足りないことだ．

別解 One problem is that we don't have enough money. **Another** problem is that we are understaffed.

問題の1つは十分なお金がないことだ．もうひとつの問題は人手不足であることだ．

To classify

分類する

ある基準に沿って，書く対象を分類する，あるいは対象を分割して1つ1つ述べていく方法です．通常は分類に使われる特定の動詞の -ed/en 形や名詞を使った後で，より具体的な情報を展開していきます．

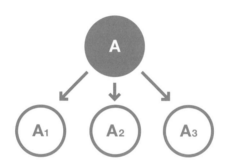

Common expressions

▶ **(is) classified as**

▶ **(is) categorized as**

▶ **consist(s) of**

▶ **(is) composed of**

▶ **(different) stages
[features, groups, includes, types, ways] (of)**

Tips to Check カテゴリーに分ける

〈トピック ＋ is/are/... classified/categorized as ＋ カテゴリー〉にして，その後にカテゴリー分けに沿った詳細を述べる方法があります．

This movie is classified as a mystery. The main character looks for his missing girlfriend while solving a few problems.

この映画はミステリーに分類される. 主人公は数々の問題を解決しながら, 失踪した彼女を探す.
- トピック ＝ この映画 ＋ カテゴリー ＝ ミステリー → ミステリーとしてのプロットの紹介

Let's Practice! 解答は次ページ

My mother is categorized ⬚ ⬚ ⬚
person. On weekdays, she enjoys talking with customers as a
sales representative. On weekends, she likes to hang out with
friends or neighbors.

母は外向的な人だ. 平日には営業として顧客と話をするのを楽しみ, 週末には友達や近所の人と付き合うの
が好きだ.
- トピック ＝ 母 ＋ カテゴリー ＝ 外向的な人 → 外向的なことを示す描写

Tips to Check より小さい 2 つ以上の構成要素に分ける

〈トピック＋ consists/is composed of ＋ 構成要素たち〉はトピックをより小さい構成要素に分類していく方法です. 当然, この構成要素は 2 つ以上になります.

My breakfast consists of two slices of toast, eggs, and
orange juice.

朝食はトースト 2 枚, 卵とオレンジジュースだ.
- トピック ＝ 朝食, 構成要素 ＝ トースト, 卵などのメニュー

Let's Practice! 解答は次ページ

A rock band is usually composed ⬚ ⬚ ⬚
—a vocalist, two guitarists, a bassist, and a drummer.

ロックバンドは通常 5 人のメンバーから構成される —— ヴォーカル, ギター 2 人, ベース, ドラム.
- トピック ＝ ロックバンド, 構成要素 ＝ 担当楽器

Tips to Check トピックの分類を予告する

分類方法に関する名詞を使い, 〈トピック＋ has ＋ 分類方法〉または〈There are ＋分類方法〉で, トピックが分類されることをまず述べてから, それぞれの分類項目を述べる方法もあります.

There are two types of leaders. The first type makes
every decision themselves. The second type shares
responsibilities with people working under them and
lets them make decisions.

2 つのタイプのリーダーがいる. 最初のタイプは決断を全部自分でする. もう 1 つのタイプは自分の下で働いている人々と責任を分かち合い, 彼らに決断を委ねる.

■ トピック ＝ リーダー, 構成要素 ＝ 2 種類のリーダー

Let's Practice!

Viruses ⬚ ⬚ ⬚ key features. These include a protective protein shell, genetic material made of nucleic acids, and an external lipid membrane.

ウイルスにはいくつかの主要な特徴がある. 保護するタンパク質の殻, 核酸で作られた遺伝子, 外側を覆っている脂質膜などである.

■ トピック ＝ ウイルス, 構成要素 ＝ ウイルスの成分

— these ＝「主要な特徴」でその後の include「含む」という動詞の後, 成分を列挙しています.

Adulthood ⬚ ⬚ distinct ⬚ : early, middle, and late. The early stage comes from 20 years old to the early 40s. The middle one occurs between one's 40s and 60s. The late stage starts from one's 60s.

成人期は初期・中期・後期の 3 つの段階に分かれる. 初期は 20 歳から始まり 40 代前半までである. 中期は 40 代から 60 代に起きる. 後期は 60 代に始まる.

解答

as an outgoing
of five members
have a few
has three / stages

Exercise

1-7 の各々が論理的に（「分類する」展開で）つながるように，空所を埋めてみましょう．必ず自分なりの解答を作ってみてください．

1 [　　　　　　] is classified as a [　　　　　　].
She/He [　　　　　　　　　　　　　　　　　]
[　　　　　　　　　　].

2 [　　　　　　　] was originally categorized as a [　　]
[　　　　]. She/He [　　　　　　　　　　　　]
[　　　　　　　　].

3 Japan consists of 47 prefectures. [　　　　　　　　]
[　　　　　　　　　　　　　　　　　　].

4 Each [　　　　　　] team is composed of [　　　]
players. Each of the [　　　　　　] is given a different role:
[　　　　　　　　　　　　　　　　　　　　].

5 People are often divided into two groups. The first group
[　　　　　　　　　　　　　　　　　　　]
[　　　　　　]. The other [　　　　　　　　]
[　　　　　　　　　　　　　　　　　　].

6 [　　　　　　] should be given tasks to [　　　　]
[　　　　　]. These types of tasks include [　　　]
[　　　　　　　　　　　　　　　　　　].

7 There are three ways to [　　　　　　]. [　　　　]
[　　　　　　　　　　　　　　　　　　].

完成したら，自分の書いたものと次ページの Sample Answers をよく比べてみましょう．

❶ Alexandria Ocasio-Cortez **is classified as** a progressive politician. She is fighting for the working class as well as for minorities.

Alexandria Ocasio-Cortez は進歩派の政治家と考えられている. 彼女は少数民族だけでなく労働者のために闘っている.

別解 Ian Bremmer **is classified as** a foreign affairs columnist. He analyzes international affairs and teaches geopolitics at a university.

Ian Bremmer は外国問題のコラムニストと考えられている. 国際問題を分析し, 大学では地政学を教えている.

❷ Taylor Swift **was** originally **categorized as** a country singer. She currently makes different genres of music.

Taylor Swift はもともとはカントリー歌手と認識されていた. 現在はさまざまなジャンルの音楽を世に出している.

別解 Steven Pinker **was** originally **categorized as** a psychologist. He is currently interested in a wide range of topics: language, the mind, and social phenomena.

Steven Pinker はもともとは心理学者という枠組みの中で認識されていた. 現在は, 言語・思考・社会現象といったたくさんの話題について関心をもっている.

❸ Japan **consists of** 47 prefectures. They are geographically divided into eight regions.

日本は 47 の都道府県からなる. その都道府県は地理的に 8 つの地域に分かれる.

別解 Japan **consists of** 47 prefectures. They include one metropolis (*to*) Tokyo, two urban prefectures (*fu*), one regional prefecture (*do*) Hokkaido, and 43 standard prefectures (*ken*).

日本は, 1 都, 2 府, 1 道, 43 県を含む 47 の都道府県からなる.

❹ Each soccer team **is composed of** eleven players. Each of the eleven is given a different role: goalkeeper, defender, midfielder, or forward.

各サッカーチームは 11 人の選手からなる. 11 人はそれぞれ異なる役割を与えられる:ゴールキーパー, ディフェンダー, ミッドフィールダー, フォワードである.

別解 Each baseball team **is composed of** nine players. Each of the nine is given a different role: pitcher, catcher, infield player, or outfield player.

各野球チームは 9 人からなる. 9 人はそれぞれ投手, 捕手, 内野手, 外野手という異なる役割を与えられる.

5 People are often divided into two groups. The first group **consists of** shy and quiet people who do not find it easy to talk to other people. The other **is of** outgoing and friendly people who like being with and talking to other people.

人は 2 つのグループに分けられる. 最初のグループは内気で静かな人で他人と話すのを苦手としている. もう 1 つのグループは外向的で気さくな, 他の人と一緒にいて話をすることが好きな人たちである.

別解 People are often divided into two groups. The first group **consists of** leaders who always make decisions themselves. The other **is of** followers who always trace the routes others map out.

人は 2 つのグループに分けられる. 最初のグループは, 自分で決断をするリーダーからなる. もう一つのグループは, いつも他人が示したルートをたどるフォロワーからなる.

6 Students should be given tasks to work on little by little without tight deadlines. These **types** of tasks include reading one novel or doing research on a particular theme using one term.

学生たちには, きつい締切のない課題を少しずつ与えるほうがよい. このタイプの課題は, 1 学期をいっぱいに使って 1 冊の小説を読んだり, 特定のテーマについて研究したりすることが例として挙げられる.

別解 Employees should be given tasks to gain a sense of accomplishment. These **types** of tasks include ones that are easy to accomplish and ones that are more challenging.

従業員には達成感が得られる課題を与えるほうがよい. このタイプの課題は, 簡単に達成できるものも, よりやりがいがあるものもある.

7 There are three **ways** to lose weight. One is to eat less. Another is to exercise more. The third is to do both.

やせるには 3 つの方法がある. 1 つは食べる量を減らすこと. もう 1 つは運動をもっとすること. 残りの 1 つは両方をすることである.

別解 There are three **ways** to reach our goal. One is to hire more people. Another is to extend the deadline. The third is to outsource a part of the project to someone else.

目標に到達するには, 3 つの方法がある. 1 つはもっと人を雇うことである. もう 1 つは締め切りを延長することである. 第 3 の方法はプロジェクトの一部を外部に委託することである.

定義する

> 「定義する」ことは前項の「分類する」に似ていますが, 「A とは B ということ」と
> 説明することです. わからない用語の意味や最も特徴的な部分を挙げることに
> よって定義はなされます.

Common expressions

▸ is called   ▸ is defined as

▸ is characterized by   ▸ is known as [for, to be]

▸ means

Tips to Check X と Y の関係に注意

One type of friendship between men is called a bromance. A bromance is platonic, or non-sexual.

男性間の友情の一種に bromance と呼ばれるものがある. bromance は純粋に精神的なもので性的な要素は
ない.

    ➤ call という動詞は〈call X Y〉〈X を Y と呼ぶ〉という使い方をしますが, 定義を与えるときには, これを受け
        身にした〈X is called Y〉というパターンがよく使われます.

Biff Tannen is characterized by his bullying in the *Back to the Future* trilogy. He is not a bright student, and he gets away with classes by having George McFly do all the course work for him.

Biff Tannen は『Back to the Future』3 部作でのいじめをする様子が特徴的だ. 彼はできる生徒ではなく,
授業の宿題を George McFly に全部やらせることで切り抜ける.

    ➤〈人 + is characterized by + 典型的な振る舞い〉は有名人や, 映画などの架空の人物のキャラクターを説
        明するときによく用いられます.

Let's Practice!

A midlife crisis means ⬚ ⬚ ⬚ when middle-aged people feel a strong desire for change. During a midlife crisis, some buy a fancy sports car, while others have a young romantic partner.

midlife crisis とは中年期の人が今までとは違ったことを急にしたがる不安定な状態のことを表わす. midlife crisis に, 派手なスポーツカーを買う人もいれば, 若い恋人を作る人もいる.

■ midlife crisis という用語の定義と説明

➤ 〈X means Y〉「X の定義は Y である」という使い方です. X も Y も名詞に相当する語句です.

⋯⋯⋯⋯⋯⋯⋯⋯⋯⋯⋯⋯⋯⋯⋯⋯⋯⋯⋯⋯⋯⋯⋯⋯⋯⋯⋯⋯⋯⋯⋯⋯⋯⋯⋯⋯

Sexual harassment is defined as ⬚ ⬚ in an unwanted, sexual manner. It includes stares, comments, and touching.

セクシュアル・ハラスメントとは, 相手が望まない形での性的な振る舞いで不快な気分にさせることと定義される. 視線や発言, 接触がこれに含まれる.

■ sexual harassment という用語の定義と具体例

➤ 〈X is defined as Y〉とすると, より辞書的な定義を与えるニュアンスが出ます.

⋯⋯⋯⋯⋯⋯⋯⋯⋯⋯⋯⋯⋯⋯⋯⋯⋯⋯⋯⋯⋯⋯⋯⋯⋯⋯⋯⋯⋯⋯⋯⋯⋯⋯⋯⋯

⬚ ⬚ is known as German Town. There used to be a lot of immigrants from Germany here.

この地域は German Town と呼ばれている. かつて, たくさんのドイツからの移民が住んでいたからだ.

■ German Town と呼ばれる理由の説明

➤ 〈X is known as Y〉は特徴を表わす「別名」を紹介するときによく使われます.

解答

the difficult period
annoying somebody
This area

Exercise

1-5 の各々が論理的に（「定義する」展開で）つながるように，空所を埋めてみましょう．必ず自分なりの解答を作ってみてください．

1 [_____] was called [_____]. She/He
[_____]
[_____].

2 [_____] is characterized by his/her [_____]
[_____]. [_____]
[_____].

3 Gaining something means losing something else. [_____]
[_____].

4 Critical thinking is loosely defined as [_____]
[_____]. It includes
identifying, analyzing, and correcting logical flaws in how
you think.

5 Sherlock Holmes is known as the greatest detective ever.
[_____]
[_____].

完成したら，自分の書いたものと次ページの Sample Answers をよく比べてみましょう．

Sample Answers

❶ Michael Jackson **was called** the King of Pop. He was an American singer, songwriter, and dancer.

Michael Jackson はポップスの帝王と呼ばれていた. 彼はアメリカ人の歌手で, 作曲家であり, ダンサーだった.

別解 Thomas Edison **was called** the Wizard of Menlo Park. He created his magical inventions in this town in New Jersey.

Thomas Edison は Menlo Park の魔術師と呼ばれていた. 彼はニュージャージーのこの街で魔法のような発明品をつくりだした.

❷ Jack Black **is characterized by** his comical behavior. He appears in a lot of comedy movies.

Jack Black はおかしな行動をすることが特徴的だ. 彼はたくさんのコメディー映画に出てくる.

別解 Olivia Rodrigo **is characterized by** her songs about unruly emotions. She rose to stardom with her debut album *Soar* and has been attracting listeners with both her catchy, distinct voice and the way she describes how life is messy.

Olivia Rodrigo は不安定な感情を描く歌が特徴的だ. 彼女はデビューアルバム『Soar』で一躍スターの階段に登った, そして, 印象的で特徴ある歌声と人生のややこしさを描いた曲で, リスナーを魅了し続けている.

❸ Gaining something **means** losing something else. In order to achieve something, you have to give up on something else you love.

何かを得ることは他の何かを失うことである. 何かを達成するためには, 大好きな他の何かを諦めなければいけない.

別解 Gaining something **means** losing something else. For example, when pop idols become really popular, they may not able to hang out with their old friends in town privately.

何かを得ることは他の何かを失うことである. たとえば, アイドルが有名になると彼らは街でこっそりと昔の友達と遊ぶことができなくなる.

❹ Critical thinking **is** loosely **defined as** <u>the ability to think in</u> <u>an organized and rational manner</u>. It includes identifying, analyzing, and correcting logical flaws in how you think.

クリティカルシンキングとは，大まかには論理的かつ合理的に頭を働かせる能力を指す．確認する，分析する，そして自分の思考における論理的な欠陥を訂正することを含む．

別解 Critical thinking **is** loosely **defined as** <u>thinking things</u> <u>through</u>. It includes identifying, analyzing, and correcting logical flows in how you think.

クリティカルシンキングとは，大まかにはものごとを考え抜くことだ．（以下，上の解答に同じ）

❺ Sherlock Holmes **is known as** the greatest detective ever. <u>He</u> <u>is a fictional character in Conan Doyle's novel series</u>.

Sherlock Holmes は史上最高の名探偵と知られている． Conan Doyle の小説に出てくる架空の人物である．

別解 Sherlock Holmes **is known as** the greatest detective ever. <u>He is good at observing and analyzing things and solves</u> <u>many difficult cases</u>.

Sherlock Holmes は史上最高の名探偵と知られている．彼はものごとの観察と分析に優れていて，多くの謎を解決する．

Chapter 1

センテンスを組み立てる

Chapter 2

センテンスをつなげる

Chapter 3

文章をまとめる

To show similarity
共通点を述べる

類似しているものを「同じく」「似たように」「比較すると」などと表現する方法です. 比較・対照 (compare & contrast) として類似点・相違点をまとめて学習することも多いですが, 本書では後者は別の項目で扱います.

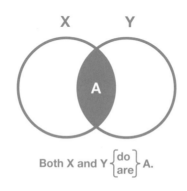

Both X and Y {do/are} A.

Common expressions

▶ also
▶ similarly
▶ likewise

▶ in the same way
▶ in the same manner
▶ in comparison

Tips to Check　too で共通点を表す

　「XもYもする／である」というとき, 以下のように too を使うのがおそらく一番簡単ですが, 別の表現も知っておく必要があります.

I hear Ted will be at this festival. Laura and Matt are coming too.

Ted がこのお祭りに来るって聞いている. Laura と Matt も来るんだ.

Let's Practice!

Conrad loves watching sports. Wayne is also ⬜ ⬜ ⬜ ⬜ sports.

Conrad はスポーツ観戦が好きだ. Wayne もスポーツが大好きだ.

- too がほとんどの場合センテンスの最後に使われるのとは対照的に, also はセンテンスの頭でも途中でも最後でも使えます. センテンスの中で使う場合, 動詞が be のときはその直後, それ以外の動詞のときはその直前に置きます (Wayne also loves watching sports.) .

Male students loosen their ties, untuck their shirts, or wear their pants below the waistline. Similarly, female students hitch their skirts way ⬜ ⬜ ⬜ .

男子生徒はネクタイをゆるめてシャツの裾を出し, 腰より下げてズボンをはく. 同じように, 女子は膝よりずっと上にスカートの裾を上げる.

- 男子生徒と女子生徒はまったく同じことをしているわけではありませんが, 制服を崩して着るという意味で似たことをしています.

Pam is the most ⬜ ⬜ ⬜ school. Likewise, Josh is the center of attention.

Pam は学校で最も人気がある女の子だ. 同じように, Josh はみんなの注目の的だ.

■ Pam と Josh の類似

Good athletes occasionally make an error. In the same way, good students sometimes ⬜ ⬜ ⬜ .

良い運動選手でも時折ミスをする. 同じように, 良い学生も間違ったことをときどきする.

■ 良い選手も良い生徒・学生もミスをする

Kevin always ⬜ ⬜ . Darin is less problematic in comparison.

Kevin はいつもトラブルを巻き起こす. それに比べると Darin の方が問題は少ない.

■ 両者とも問題を起こすという共通点がある前提での比較

解答

a big fan of	do something wrong
above their knees	causes trouble
popular girl at	

Exercise

1-6 の各々が論理的に (「共通点を述べる」展開で) つながるように, 空所を埋めてみましょう. 必ず自分なりの解答を作ってみてください.

1. Melissa is a very nice lady. She [＿＿＿＿＿＿＿＿＿＿] too.

2. Kids do not always focus on outperforming others. They also [＿＿＿＿＿＿＿＿＿＿＿＿＿＿＿].

3. In Japan, the number of female police officers is increasing. Similarly, [＿＿＿＿＿＿＿＿＿＿＿＿＿].

4. Kids feel envy or unhappiness when other children perform better than them. Likewise, [＿＿＿＿＿＿＿＿] [＿＿＿＿＿＿＿＿＿＿＿＿＿＿].

5. Good leaders listen to people working under them. In the same manner, [＿＿＿＿＿＿＿＿＿＿＿＿] [＿＿＿＿＿＿＿＿＿＿＿＿＿＿].

6. Gayla always stands out. Catherine [＿＿＿＿＿＿＿＿＿] in comparison.

完成したら, 自分の書いたものと次ページの Sample Answers をよく比べてみましょう.

┤ Sample Answers ├

❶ Melissa is a very nice lady. She is very smart **too**.

Melissa はとても親切な女性だ. 彼女はとても頭も良い.

別解 Melissa is a very nice lady. She has a good sense of humor **too**.

Melissa はとても親切な女性だ. 彼女はユーモアのセンスもある.

❷ Kids do not always focus on outperforming others. They **also** think about offering help and solving problems as a team.

子どもたちはいつも他人を出し抜くことを重視しているわけではない. 彼らは手を差し伸べることや仲間と一緒に問題を解決することも考えている.

別解 Kids do not always focus on outperforming others. They **also** like to work with others and share fun time together.

子どもたちはいつも他人を出し抜くことを重視しているわけではない. 彼らは他人と一緒に作業をして, 喜びを分かち合うこともする.

❸ In Japan, the number of female police officers is increasing. **Similarly**, there are more and more male nurses.

日本では女性警察官の数が増えている. 同じように, 男性看護師の数も増えている.

別解 In Japan, the number of female police officers is increasing. **Similarly**, more and more women are starting their own businesses.

日本では女性警察官の数が増えている. 同じように, 起業する女性も増えている.

❹ Kids feel envy or unhappiness when other children perform better than them. **Likewise**, they feel good when they outperform others.

子どもは他の子どもが自分よりもすぐれたことをやってみせるとうらやむ. 同じように, 自分が他人よりも上回っているときに気分が良くなる.

別解 Kids feel envy or unhappiness when other children perform better than them. **Likewise**, achieving better results than others could give them a feeling of superiority.

子どもは他の子どもが自分よりもすぐれたことをやってみせるとうらやむ. 同じように, 他人よりもよい結果を得ることは, 優越感を得ることにもつながる.

⑤ Good leaders listen to people working under them. **In the same manner,** Mr. Tanaka often asks other people's opinions during the Monday briefings.

すぐれた指導者は自分の下で働いている人の話を聞く．同じように，Tanaka さんは月曜日の会議で他の人の意見をたずねる．

別解 Good leaders listen to people working under them. **In the same manner,** good football coaches decide what and how to practice while also discussing their strategies with players.

すぐれた指導者は自分の下で働いている人の話を聞く．同じように，よいフットボールの監督は選手と戦術を練りながら，何をどのように練習するかを決める．

⑥ Gayla always stands out. Catherine gets less attention **in comparison.**

Gayla はいつも目立っている．それに比べれば，Catherine は周囲の注目が少ない．

別解 Gayla always stands out. Catherine tends to remain unnoticed **in comparison.**

Gayla はいつも目立っている．それに比べれば，Catherine は目立たないままに終わりがちだ．

Chapter 1　センテンスを組み立てる

Chapter 2　センテンスをつなげる

Chapter 3　文章をまとめる

To show contrast or indicate an unexpected result

対比や逆接・意外な展開を示す

前項とは違って，今度は前後 2 つの人・もの・ことが異なっていたり，逆になっているときの表現を扱います．

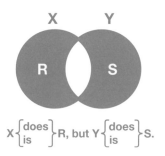

$$X \left\{ \begin{array}{l} \text{does} \\ \text{is} \end{array} \right\} R, \text{ but } Y \left\{ \begin{array}{l} \text{does} \\ \text{is} \end{array} \right\} S.$$

Common expressions

- ▸ however
- ▸ though
- ▸ nevertheless
- ▸ in contrast
- ▸ on the other hand
- ▸ on the contrary
- ▸ instead
- ▸ conversely
- ▸ still
- ▸ now

　逆接や対比というと，but, although, while などを思い浮かべるかもしれませんが，これらはもっぱらセンテンスの中で使われ，センテンスを超えた内容のつながりを表わすときには使えません．

Examples

Danny firmly believes he works the hardest on the team, but his coworkers would never feel that way.

Danny はチームの中で自分が一番働いていると信じて疑わないが，彼の同僚たちは決してそうは感じていない．

Although Kate started working as a model for the money, the job has helped her make friends with actors and designers.

Kate はお金のためにモデルとして働き始めたが, この仕事は彼女が役者やデザイナーと仲良くなるのに役立っている.

While Lori casually speaks with new people, Brian often stays silent.

Lori は気軽に新しい人に話しかけるが, Brian は黙っていることが多い.

 Tips to Check つなぎ言葉は文頭・文中・文尾でも使える

一番よく使われるのは however です.

In soccer, players kick a ball to move it toward their opponent's goal. In baseball, however, a batter hits a thrown ball with a bat into a field area and make it around four bases to score.

サッカーでは競技者は相手のゴールに向かってボールを蹴る. 一方, 野球では打者は投げられたボールをバットでフェアゾーンに入れて, 得点するのに 4 つのベースを回る.
■ 野球とサッカーの対比
➤ however は文頭・文中・文尾のいずれでも使われ, 意味的にも「ところが」のように前とまったく逆のことを展開するときにも,「だが一方」のように異なる要素の対比にも使えます.

We all wanted to know what had happened between Sally and Matt on that day. We were hardly interested in whether they would get back together or not, though.

私たちはみんなその日 Sally と Matt の間に何があったのかを知りたいんだ. でも, 彼らがよりを戻すかどうかにはあまり関心がない.
■ 関心があることとないことの対比
➤ though は文中でも使えますが, 文尾で使うことが圧倒的に多いです.「だけれど」という前に述べられたこととは相入れないことを一応言っておく, という弱いニュアンスの表現です.

What Jessica said to her boss was extremely inappropriate. Nevertheless, many of her colleagues felt for her.

Jessica が上司に言ったことは大変不適切だ. それでも, 多くの同僚は彼女に同情した.
■ ジェシカの発言の不適切さと同僚の反応の対比
➤ nevertheless は前に否定的な内容があるのに「それでも」というニュアンスを出すときに使われます.

Chapter 1 センテンスを組み立てる

Chapter 2 センテンスをつなげる

Chapter 3 文章をまとめる

Kahoko and Satoshi show different types of leadership. Kahoko tends to decide everything herself and tells others to follow what she decides. <u>In contrast</u>, Satoshi often lets other people make decisions and offers helps only when asked.

Kahoko と Satoshi は別の種類のリーダーシップを発揮する。Kahoko は自分で何でも決める傾向があり，決めたことを他人に従うように言う。対照的に，Satoshi は他の人たちに決めさせて，求められたときにだけ手助けをする。

■ 2 人のリーダーシップの取り方の比較

⊢ 2 つのものを比較して違いを述べるときは in contrast を使います。

Let's Practice!

Eating healthy food helps you stay in good shape. On the other hand, ☐☐☐☐ can harm your physical and mental health.

健康的なものを食べているとずっとよい体調を維持できる。逆に，栄養価の低いものばかり食べていると体と精神を悪くしてしまう。

■ 健康な食生活と不健康な食生活の対比

⋯⋯⋯⋯⋯⋯⋯⋯⋯⋯⋯⋯⋯⋯⋯⋯⋯⋯⋯⋯⋯⋯⋯⋯⋯⋯⋯

Most teammates were very optimistic. Jo and I, on the contrary, felt that we were going to ☐☐☐ ☐☐ the next day.

ほとんどのチームメイトはとても楽観的だった。それどころか，Jo と私は翌日はきつい試合になると感じていた。

■ チームメイトの感覚と Jo と私の感覚との対比

⋯⋯⋯⋯⋯⋯⋯⋯⋯⋯⋯⋯⋯⋯⋯⋯⋯⋯⋯⋯⋯⋯⋯⋯⋯⋯⋯

Children with a short attention span should be ☐ ☐☐ anything eye-catchy, from social media or video streaming services to text messaging apps. Instead, they should be given tasks to work on little by little without tight deadlines.

集中力のない子どもは SNS でも映像視聴サービスでもチャットアプリでも，目立つものからは遠ざけておいた方がいい。代わりに，彼らにはきつい締切がなく少しずつ取り組める課題を与えるとよい。

■ 子どもに与えない方がよいものと与えた方がよいものの対比

⊢ 代用，代替案を出すときに使う単語です。

Between 2001 and 2010, a large number of retired people moved into Warrensburg. Conversely, many young people [_____] [_____] [_____] because they could not find jobs there.

2001 年から 2010 年の間，多くの退職者たちが Warrensburg に引っ越してきた．逆に，仕事が見つけられず多くの若者がこの街を去っていった．

■ 退職した人と若者の行動における対比

The food at the French restaurant was horrible. Still, I [_____] [_____] my boyfriend on that day.

そのフランス料理店の食事はひどくまずかった．それでも，その日彼氏と会うことができてよかった．

■ 同日に起きた悪い体験と良い体験の対比

➤ nevertheless と同じで否定的な内容の後に使う単語です．

Shinichi used to dislike English, and he often skipped English classes in college. Now as the owner of an IT venture business, he [_____] [_____] customers in English every day.

Shinichi は英語が嫌いで，大学ではよく英語の授業をサボっていた．今や彼は IT ベンチャー企業の社長で，顧客と毎日英語でやりとりをしている．

■ 過去と現在の対比

解答

consuming a poor diet
have a very tough game
kept away from
left the town
enjoyed meeting
communicates with

Exercise

1-9 の各々が論理的に（「対比」「逆接」の展開で）つながるように，空所を埋めてみましょう. 必ず自分なりの解答を作ってみてください.

1 [   ]
[   ]. What he has in mind, however, is beyond our imagination.

2 Roger disappointed Laura many times. Nevertheless, [   ].

3 The two girls have different [   ]. Miu [   ] [   ]. In contrast, Hitomi's [   ].

4 Danny is considered a troublemaker. On the other hand, Jeff [   ].

5 Giving advice to younger people about their lifestyles or behaviors will not help you become popular. On the contrary, [   ].

6 [   ]. Instead, it can also make us more stressed.

7 Introverts [   ] [   ]. Conversely, extroverts [   ] [   ].

8 Most people have already given up hope in making this project successful. Still, [   ].

9 Suzuka used to be isolated. [   ] [   ] now.

完成したら, 自分の書いたものと次ページの Sample Answers をよく比べてみましょう.

Sample Answers

1 We have worked closely with Mr. Armstrong for more than 10 years. What he has in mind, **however**, is beyond our imagination.

私たちは Armstrong さんと 10 年以上にわたって一緒に仕事をしてきたが，彼の考えていることは私たちの想像を超える．

別解 We all know how unique Mr. Armstrong is and always try to be ready for whatever he comes up with. What he has in mind, **however**, is beyond our imagination.

Armstrong さんがどれだけユニークな人間かを，みんな心得ていて，彼が思いつくことは何でも受け入れようとしているが，彼の考えていることは私たちの想像を超える．

2 Roger disappointed Laura many times. **Nevertheless**, she decided to stay with him.

Roger は何度も Laura をがっかりさせた．それでも，彼女は彼と一緒にいることを選んだ．

別解 Roger disappointed Laura many times. **Nevertheless**, she wouldn't stop trusting him.

Roger は何度も Laura をがっかりさせた．それでも，彼女は彼を信じることをやめようとはしない．

3 The two girls have different hairstyles. Miu has long, black, and wavy hair. **In contrast**, Hitomi's hair is short, brown, and straight.

2 人の女の子は違う髪型をしている．　Miu は長くて，黒いウェーヴのかかった髪をしている．それに対して，Hitomi は短くて，茶色のストレートの髪だ．

別解 The two girls have different personalities. Miu needs time to make friends with new people. **In contrast**, Hitomi's outgoing personality helps her find new friends quickly.

2 人の女の子は違う性格をしている．Miu は出会った人と仲良くなるのに時間がかかる．それに対して，Hitomi は外向的で，新しい友達がすぐにできる．

4 Danny is considered a troublemaker. **On the other hand**, Jeff is a role model for the team.

Danny は問題児だと思われている．一方，Jeff はチームの模範だ．

別解 Danny is considered a troublemaker. **On the other hand**, Jeff is trusted by everybody.

Danny は問題児だと思われている．一方，Jeff はみんなから信用されている．

5 Giving advice to younger people about their lifestyles or behaviors will not help you become popular. **On the contrary, you will probably be considered annoying.**

若者の生き方や行動について忠告をしても，あなたの株は上がらない．逆に，うるさいやつだと思われる．

別解 Giving advice to younger people about their lifestyles or behaviors will not help you become popular. **On the contrary**, these youngsters will regard you as a thoughtless, stubborn old person.

若者の生き方や行動について忠告をしても，あなたの株は上がらない．逆に，これらの若い人たちはあなたを考えの浅い強情な古い人間とみなすだろう．

6 Technology doesn't always make our life comfortable. **Instead,** it can also make us more stressed.

科学技術は私たちの暮らしをいつも快適にするわけではない．ストレスになることだってある．

別解 Money doesn't always bring happiness. **Instead**, it can also make us more stressed.

お金は必ずしも幸せをもたらすとは限らない．ストレスになることだってある．

7 Introverts tend to have difficulty working with new people. **Conversely**, extroverts perform well when they do tasks with other people.

内向的な人は新しい人とやっていくことを苦手としがちだ．逆に，外向的な人は他の人たちと仕事をするとパフォーマンスが向上する．

別解 Introverts prefer being with a limited number of familiar people. **Conversely**, extroverts don't mind being around those who they don't know well.

内向的な人は，少数のよく知った人と一緒にいるのが好きだ．逆に，外向的な人というのは、知らない人に囲まれても全然気にしない．

8 Most people have already given up hope in making this project successful. **Still**, Jessica is holding out for a miracle.

ほとんどの人はこのプロジェクトがうまくいかないと，すでに諦めているが，Jessica はまだ奇跡が起こる可能性を諦めない．

別解 Most people have already given up hope in making this project successful. **Still**, a few live in hope.

ほとんどの人はこのプロジェクトがうまくいかないと，すでに諦めているが，何人かは望みを捨てきれない．

❾ Suzuka used to be isolated. <u>She is the center of attention</u> **now**.

Suzuka はかつて孤立していた. 今や注目の的だ.

別解 Suzuka used to be isolated. <u>She is surrounded by a group of people</u> **now**.

Suzuka はかつて孤立していた. 今や彼女は人の群れに囲まれている.

因果関係を示す

文章の中で原因（cause）と結果（effect）を正しく述べることは，論理的に表現する上で非常に大事です．しかし，多くの英語学習者が因果関係を逆にしたり，存在しない因果関係を述べてしまいます．

Tips to Check 論理的な破綻は NG

　因果関係を表す because は英語学習者なら誰でも知っている基本語です．

　しかし，英語に自信がない人はもちろん，中級・上級者でも複数のセンテンスを重ねて因果関係を表そうとすると，かなりの学習者が以下のように書いてしまいます．

✗ I love the man because, he is my boyfriend.

　　彼は彼氏なので，私は彼を愛している．

　〈S＋V＋... because S＋V＋...〉あるいは〈Because S＋V＋..., S＋V＋...〉としなければいけないという形の問題もありますが，より問題なのは論理的に破綻していることです．「彼氏だから好き」というのは変な理屈で，

I decided to go out with the man because I liked him.

彼のことが好きだったので付き合うことにした．

I have come to love the man more since we started going out.

付き合い始めたら，その人のことがより好きになった．

などとするべきでしょう．

Let's Practice!

✘ I think going to school is fun, because it's fun to go to school for me.

私は学校に行くのが楽しいので，通学とは楽しいことだと思う．

　まず，「楽しい」から「楽しい」というのは論理として成り立ちません．日常生活ではそのように強引に意見を通すこともあり得ますが，ライティングの世界ではだめです．さらに，going to school is fun というのは一般論の意見のはずですが，fun to go to school for me という自分個人にあてはまることを根拠にするのは論理的ではありません．

I think going to school is fun because ⬚⬚⬚⬚⬚⬚⬚⬚⬚⬚⬚⬚⬚⬚⬚⬚⬚⬚⬚ .

教室内でも教室外でもたくさんのことが学べるから学校に行くのは楽しい．
■ 何が楽しいかを具体的に

✘ Math and science are important because they are important subjects.

数学と理科は私にとって重要な教科なので，重要なものだと思う．

　これも「重要科目だから重要です」では論理に無理があります．

Math and science are important ⬚⬚⬚⬚⬚⬚⬚⬚⬚⬚⬚⬚⬚⬚⬚⬚⬚⬚⬚ .

周りにあるものがどのように体系づけられているのかを子どもたちが理解する手助けをするのに役に立つので，数学や理科は大事だ．
■ 何が重要かを具体的に

解答例

you can learn so many things both inside and outside the classroom
because they help kids understand how things around them are organized

Exercise

次の 1-3 は文法的・内容的に誤りがあります. 意味が通るように書き換えてください.
必ず自分なりの答えを作ってみてください.

1 ✗ High school students have to study because study is a duty for them.

2 ✗ The police think that the woman is doubtful. Because, they didn't trust what she said.

3 ✗ *Ferris Bueller's Day Off* is my favorite movie. Because, I like the movie so much.

完成したら, 自分の書いたものと次の Sample Answers をよく比べてみましょう.

Sample Answers

1 High school students <u>should focus on studying rather than working part-time because what they learn at school will benefits them when they work full-time in the future</u>.

高校生はアルバイトよりも勉強に集中した方がいい. その理由は, 学校で学ぶことは将来定職に就いたときに役に立つからである.

2 The police think that the woman is doubtful <u>because what she told them was inconsistent</u>.

警察はその女は怪しいと考えている. なぜなら警察に彼女が語った内容は首尾一貫していないからだ.

3 *Ferris Bueller's Day Off* is my favorite movie <u>because it reminds me of my high school days full of stupidity and fun</u>.

『フェリスはある朝突然に』は私の大好きな映画である. それはばかばかしくて面白かった私の高校時代を思い起こさせるからだ.

Common expressions

▶ this is because

▶ the reason is that

▶ as a result

▶ therefore

▶ thus

▶ consequently

▶ for this reason

▶ accordingly

▶ in effect

因果関係は 2 文以上が効果的

ここまでは 1 つのセンテンス内での因果関係の表現法ですが，ライティングでは因果関係は 2 つ以上のセンテンスで表現した方が効果的です．「結果 → 原因」の順で展開する場合には，センテンス間に何も入れなくても自然に意味が通じることがほとんどです．入れる場合は this is because / the reason is that を使います．

High school students have to study what they are poor at as well as what they are good at. Gaining wide knowledge will expand their worldview.

高校生は自分が得意なことだけでなく苦手なことも勉強しないといけない．広い知識を身につけることが彼らの世界観を広げる．

Children should be given plenty of time to play. This is because they learn how to work with others through play.

子どもたちはたくさん遊ぶ時間が与えられた方がよい．というのは，遊びを通じて子どもは他人と一緒に何かをするということを学ぶからだ．

Let's Practice!

Financial management should be taught at school. ☐
☐ .

お金の管理は学校で教えられた方がいい．生活に最も必要なスキルの 1 つだからだ．
■ 接続の表現ナシ

The police suspect that Mr. Crawford committed the crime. The reason is that ☐ ☐ ☐ ☐ ☐ .

警察はクロフォード氏がその罪を犯したと疑っている．なぜなら彼にはアリバイがないからだ．
■ 接続の表現アリ

解答例

It is one of the most important life skills
he doesn't have an alibi

Exercise

1-7 の各々が論理的に（「意見→理由」の展開で）つながるように，空所を埋めてみましょう．必ず自分なりの解答を作ってみてください．

1 The Olympic Games should be abolished. _____
_____.

2 Young people should listen to older people. _____
_____.

3 It is absolutely wrong to lie. _____
_____.

4 The detective did not believe Yolanda. _____
_____.

5 Vending machines should not be banned. They _____
_____.

6 These days few women quit work after they have children.
This is because _____
_____.

7 Jeremy hardly talks about his parents. The reason is that _____
_____.

完成したら，自分の書いたものと次ページの Sample Answers をよく比べてみましょう．

Sample Answers

❶ The Olympic Games should be abolished. These days, they don't help to promote world peace.

オリンピックは廃止した方がよい. 近頃は, 平和を促進するのに役に立っていない.

別解 The Olympic Games should be abolished. They force host countries to make huge investments.

オリンピックは廃止した方がよい. 開催国にたくさんの投資を行なわせる.

❷ Young people should listen to older people. Listening to those who have lived longer helps them avoid making the same mistakes.

若い人は年配の人のいうことを聞いた方がよい. 長く生きた人の話を聞くことは, 自分が同じ間違いを避けるのに役立つ.

別解 Young people should listen to older people. They have a lifetime of experience and want to help those who are just starting out.

若い人は年配の人のいうことを聞いた方がよい. 彼らには人生経験があり, まだ人生のスタート地点付近にいる人たちを助けたいのだから.

❸ It is absolutely wrong to lie. Lying inevitably hurts other people.

嘘をつくのは絶対によくない. 嘘は他人を必ず傷つけるからだ.

別解 It is absolutely wrong to lie. People may suffer from not knowing the truth, and this will give you pain.

嘘をつくのは絶対によくない. 人々は真実を知らないことで苦しむことがあり, そのことによってあなたが苦痛を味わう.

❹ The detective did not believe Yolanda. She said she left work at six, but her colleagues denied it.

その刑事は Yolanda の言うことを信じなかった. 6 時に会社を出たと言ったが, 彼女の同僚はそれを否定した.

別解 The detective did not believe Yolanda. She insisted that she didn't know the victim, but she had been seen with him many times.

その刑事は Yolanda の言うことを信じなかった. 彼女は被害者を知らないと主張したが, 彼といるところを何度も目撃されている.

5 Vending machines should not be banned. They are convenient for both beverage companies and customers.

自動販売機はなくすべきではない. 飲料会社にも顧客にも便利だからだ.

別解 Vending machines should not be banned. They are needed for people without a convenience store nearby.

自動販売機はなくすべきではない. それらはコンビニが近くにない人にとっては必要とされているのだ.

6 These days few women quit work after they have children. This is because more and more companies provide better working environments for them.

近頃では子どもを産んでから退職する女性が少なくなった. だんだん多くの会社が良い労働環境を提供するようになってきたからだ.

別解 These days few women quit work after they have children. This is because they can't get by on only their husbands' salaries.

近頃では子どもを産んでから退職する女性が少なくなった. 彼女たちは夫の給料だけではやっていけないのだ.

7 Jeremy hardly talks about his parents. The reason is that he doesn't get along well with them.

Jeremy はほとんど自分の両親について話さない. 彼らとうまくいっていないからだ.

別解 Jeremy hardly talks about his parents. The reason is that both of them have already passed away.

Jeremy はほとんど自分の両親について話さない. 両親とも他界してしまったからだ.

Tips to Check 「原因→結果」の表現

「原因 → 結果」の場合，話し言葉ならばこのような表現法も可能です．

Ashley often badmouthed her colleagues. So, nobody at her workplace liked her.

Ashley はよく同僚の悪口を言うので，職場の誰も彼女のことが好きでない．

■ So の後でひと息入れないときは，Ashley often badmouthed her colleagues. So nobody at her workplace liked her. となります．小学生の作文やカジュアルな場面ではアメリカ人もよく使います．アカデミックライティングでは，Ashley often badmouthed her colleagues, so nobody at her workplace liked her. のようにセンテンスの中で使うように指導されることが多いです．

Ms. Donaldson can't drive. That's why she did not kill her husband.

Donaldson 夫人は運転できない．このことから，彼女は夫を殺していないとわかる．

Everybody at the office was extremely unfriendly and rude to me. This is why I quit.

会社のみんなは私に対してとても冷淡で失礼だった．それが私が辞めた理由だ．

Ian used to work at Rachel's bakery. Because of this, he knows her well.

Ian は Rachel のパン屋で働いていたことがある．だから，彼は彼女のことをよく知っている．

Let's Practice!

次に，書き言葉向きの表現が含まれた例を練習してみましょう．

We did the best we could. As a result, ☐ ☐ ☐
☐.

私たちは最善を尽くした．その結果，決勝戦に勝った．

What Ms. Marcus says does not make sense. Therefore, not many people ☐ ☐ ☐.

Marcus さんの言うことは意味不明だ．それゆえ，彼女のいうことを聞く人はほとんどいない．

Nobody opposed Jason's plan. Thus, ☐ ☐
☐.

誰も Jason の案に反対しなかった．こうして，それは採用された．

■ それ＝ Jason の案

Chapter 1 センテンスを組み立てる

Chapter 2 センテンスをつなげる

Chapter 3 文章をまとめる

Mr. Douglas wanted to spend more time with his family. For this reason, he [   ] [   ] the position of CEO.

Douglas さんは家族との時間を増やしたかった. このため, 会長の職を退いた.

....

The country's economy is pretty bad. Consequently, many young people can't [   ] [   ] [   ] job.

この国の経済状態はひどく悪い. その結果, 多くの若者が定職を見つけられないでいる.

....

The school got a number of complaints from students about the quality of the food at its cafeteria. Accordingly, [   ] [   ] [   ] change vendors.

その学校は食堂の料理の質について学生からたくさんの苦情を受けた. その結果, 業者を替えることにした.

....

Students have to iron and dry clean their uniforms. In effect, [   ] [   ] [   ] them busier.

学生は制服にアイロンをかけたりドライクリーニングしないといけない. その結果, 制服を着ることが, 彼らの時間を奪っている.

■ 彼らの時間を奪う＝彼らをより忙しくさせる

解答

we won the championship
listen to her
it was adopted
retired from
get a full-time
it decided to
wearing uniforms makes

096

Exercise

1-6 の各々が論理的に（「因果関係」の展開で）つながるように，空所を埋めてみましょう. 必ず自分なりの解答を作ってみてください.

1 Lily badmouthed her coworkers and spread false rumors about them. As a result, she _____
_____.

2 A few members caused trouble. Therefore, _____
_____.

3 It is snowing really heavily. Thus, _____
_____.

4 Most young people have left this town. Consequently, _____
_____.

5 Some parents insisted that their kids should learn art as well as science. Accordingly, _____
_____.

6 Jesse couldn't find a job at any other place. In effect, _____
_____.

完成したら, 自分の書いたものと次ページの Sample Answers をよく比べてみましょう.

❶ Lily badmouthed her coworkers and spread false rumors about them. **As a result**, she lost support from everyone at her workplace.

Lily は同僚の悪口を言って嘘の噂話を広げた. 結果として, 職場の誰からも助けが得られなくなった.

別解 Lily badmouthed her coworkers and spread false rumors about them. **As a result**, she doesn't have anyone to speak with now.

Lily は同僚の悪口を言って嘘の噂話を広げた. 結果として, 彼女には話し相手はもう誰もいない.

❷ A few members caused trouble. **Therefore**, the team had to withdraw from the prefectural tournament.

数人の部員が問題を起こした. 結果として, そのチームは県大会への出場を諦めなくてはならなかった.

別解 A few members caused trouble. **Therefore**, all of us are considered to be troublemakers.

数人の部員が問題を起こした. 結果として, 私たちみんながトラブルメーカーだと考えられている.

❸ It is snowing really heavily. **Thus**, some train delays are expected.

ひどい雪が降っている. そのため, 電車の遅れが予想される.

別解 It is snowing really heavily. **Thus**, it could pile up outside.

ひどい雪が降っている. そのため, 積もる可能性がある.

❹ Most young people have left this town. **Consequently**, only elderly people are left.

ほとんどの若者はこの街を去った. 結果として老人だけが残った.

別解 Most young people have left this town. **Consequently**, all restaurants and stores, except for those operated by elderly people, are closed.

ほとんどの若者はこの街を去った. 結果として, お年寄りがやっているものを除いて, すべてのレストランや商店が営業をやめてしまった.

5 Some parents insisted that their kids should learn art as well as science. **Accordingly**, some art classes were added to the curriculum.

> 親たちは自分の子どもが科学科目だけでなく芸術科目も学んだ方がよいと主張した. その結果, いくつかの芸術科目がカリキュラムに追加された.

別解 Some parents insisted that their kids should learn art as well as science. **Accordingly**, the school decided to open music, theater, and fine art classes in the next school year.

> 親たちは自分の子どもが科学科目だけでなく芸術科目も学んだ方がよいと主張した. その結果, その学校は来年度から音楽, 演劇, 美術のクラスを開講することに決めた.

6 Jesse couldn't find a job at any other place. **In effect**, he had to accept his salary cut and remain at the company.

> Jesse は他の場所で仕事を見つけることができなかった. 結果として, 彼は給料のカットを受け入れて会社に残るしかなかった.

別解 Jesse couldn't find a job at any other place. **In effect**, not a single company even contacted him to schedule an interview.

> Jesse は他の場所で仕事を見つけることができなかった. それどころか, たった 1 社も彼に面接をするために連絡をとろうとはしなかった.

> ➤ in effect は前に書かれてことを受けてその結果はこういうことなんだというニュアンスで因果関係を表すこともできますが, 意味としては Section 12 で扱われる「実際」(= in fact), 「本質的には」(= in essence) なので, このような使い方も可能です.

To give an example

例を挙げる

自分の意見や考え・現象をざっくりと述べただけでは不十分で，場合によっては具体例を出してよりわかりやすく納得させる必要があります．

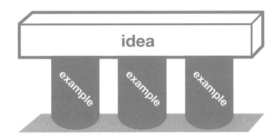

Common expressions

▸ for example

▸ for instance

▸ in particular

▸ typically

▸ specifically

▸ to illustrate

Tips to Check つなぎ言葉の後の内容が大事

例を挙げるためのつなぎに使われる表現もありますが，より大事なことはつなぎ表現の後の具体例の質です．例になっていないものを使っていないか，例ではあるものの前に書いてあることを説明したり納得させるのに十分かどうかをよく考えましょう．

Things have changed a lot since our parents were young. For example, when my mother was about my age, the economy was extremely good.

私の両親が若い頃と比べて世の中は大きく変わった．例えば，私の母が私ぐらいのとき，景気はとても良かった．
■ 変化の具体例として景気

Let's Practice!

Some of the people who failed to show up at the event had no alibis. For instance, Ms. Smith says she ☐ ☐ ☐ ☐ at the time, but she has no one to prove it.

そのイベントに出席できなかった人たちの中にはアリバイがない人もいた. 例えば, Smith さんはその時間病気で家で寝ていたと言っているが, 誰もそれを証明できない.

■ アリバイのない人の具体例として Smith さん

There were a few players ☐ ☐ ☐. In particular, Seth Powell hit three singles.

何人か活躍した選手もいる. とりわけ, Seth Powell は 3 つのシングルヒットを打った.

■ 活躍した選手の具体例として Seth Powell

Inspector Lestrade questioned me ☐ very ☐ ☐. Specifically, he had me answer who I liked or disliked and whether I was in a romantic relationship with somebody in the class.

Lestrade 警部は私のとても個人的なことについて尋問した. とりわけ, 親しい人, 仲が悪い人や, クラスの誰かと恋愛関係にないか答えを求めた.

■ 個人的な事柄の具体例

Team sports teach children much more than just athletic skills. To illustrate, look at how the members of the basketball team have ☐ ☐ ☐ and communication skills over the season.

団体競技は子どもたちに運動能力以上のものを身につけさせる. バスケ部の部員がシーズンを通じてチームワークやコミュニケーション能力を向上させた例を見てみよう.

■ 運動能力以外の子どもの学びの具体例

解答

was sick at home
who performed well
on / personal matters
improved their teamwork

Exercise

1-8の各々が論理的に（「例を挙げる」展開で）つながるように，空所を埋めてみましょう．必ず自分なりの解答を作ってみてください．

1 [＿＿＿＿＿＿＿＿＿] makes tiny, stupid mistakes almost every day. For example, [＿＿＿＿＿＿＿＿＿]
[＿＿＿＿＿＿＿＿＿].

2 David Edison often asks people difficult questions. For example, he asked [＿＿＿＿＿＿＿＿＿]
[＿＿＿＿＿＿＿＿＿].

3 Unexpected outcomes sometimes occur from online meetings. For example, [＿＿＿＿＿＿＿＿＿]
[＿＿＿＿＿＿＿＿＿]
[＿＿＿＿＿＿＿＿＿].

4 Some famous people openly talk about social issues. For instance, [＿＿＿＿＿＿＿＿＿]
[＿＿＿＿＿＿＿＿＿]
[＿＿＿＿＿].

5 People can achieve their dreams even in old age. As an example, [＿＿＿＿＿＿＿＿＿].

6 The detective asked the girl many questions. In particular, [＿＿＿＿＿＿＿＿＿].

7 We had strict rules about how to wear uniforms. Specifically, [＿＿＿＿＿＿＿＿＿]
[＿＿＿＿＿＿＿＿＿].

Section **10**
例を挙げる

Chapter 1
センテンスを組み立てる

Chapter 2
センテンスをつなげる

Chapter 3
文章をまとめる

8 Some people don't believe the old maxim "honesty pays."
To illustrate, ⎸＿＿＿＿＿＿＿＿＿＿＿＿＿＿＿＿＿＿＿⎹

＿＿＿＿＿＿＿＿＿＿＿＿＿＿＿＿＿＿＿＿＿＿＿

⎸＿＿＿＿＿＿⎹ .

完成したら，自分の書いたものと次の Sample Answers をよく比べてみましょう.

──[Sample Answers]────────────────────────

① My mother makes tiny, stupid mistakes almost every day. **For example**, this morning, the coffee tasted terrible and we found that she had put mayonnaise and salt instead of cream and sugar into it.

母はほぼ毎日小さなばかな間違いをする. 例えば，今朝コーヒーの味が変なので見ると，クリームと砂糖の代わりにマヨネーズと塩を入れていた.

別解 My younger sister makes tiny, stupid mistakes almost every day. **For example**, this morning, she hurried to school with her pajamas on, stumbled on the pavement, and fell three times.

わたしの妹は，ほぼ毎日小さなばかな間違いをする. 例えば，今朝，彼女は寝巻きで学校に急いで，舗道でつまづいて，3回転んだ.

② David Edison often asks people difficult questions. **For example**, he asked me over lunch yesterday, "What is the purpose of your life?"

David Edison はよく人々に難しい質問を浴びせる. 例えば，昨日の昼食の時，彼は私に「君の人生の目的って何?」と聞いてきた.

別解 David Edison often asks people difficult questions. **For example**, he asked me how I should act to make the world a better place.

David Edison はよく人々に難しい質問を浴びせる. 例えば，私にどのようにして世の中を良くしようと行動するのが望ましいか尋ねてきた.

❸ Unexpected outcomes sometimes occur from online meetings. **For example**, my younger sister got to know a man on social media, met him in person, and married him a few months later.

オンライン上で予期せぬ出会いが起きることがある．例えば，私の妹は SNS である男性に初めて出会い，実際に会って，数ヶ月後に結婚した．

> 別解 Unexpected outcomes sometimes occur from online meetings. **For example**, I got to know that I was dating my boss's daughter when I had a video chat with him while he was at his house.
>
> オンライン上で予期せぬ出会いが起きることがある．例えば，私は自宅にいる上司とオンライン会議をしたときに，上司の娘とつきあっていることに気づいてしまった．

❹ Some famous people openly talk about social issues. **For instance**, the actress Alicia Silverstone has been a vegan and animal rights advocate for more than twenty years.

有名人の中には社会問題についてオープンに発言する人もいる．女優の Alicia Silverstone は 20 年以上にわたってヴィーガンで動物愛護の支持者である．

> 別解 Some famous people openly talk about social issues. **For instance**, actress Emma Watson has been vocal about women's rights.
>
> 有名人の中には社会問題についてオープンに発言する人もいる．例えば，女優の Emma Watson は女性の権利について声を上げている．

❺ People can achieve their dreams even in old age. **As an example**, my mom formed a punk rock band with some of her coworkers and held a concert at a big hall last year.

年を取ってからも夢を実現することは可能だ．例えば，私の母は会社の同僚とロックバンドを結成し，昨年大きなホールでライブを開催した．

> 別解 People can achieve their dreams even in old age. **As an example**, Seicho Matsumoto made his debut as a writer at the age of 42, wrote many famous mystery stories, and became recognized as one of Japan's greatest writers.
>
> 年を取ってからも夢を実現することは可能だ．例えば，Seicho Matsumoto は 42 歳で作家としてデビューしてたくさんの推理小説を書き，日本を代表する作家と呼ばれるまでになった．

6 The detective asked the girl many questions. **In particular**, he wanted to know how close she was to the victim.

刑事は少女にたくさんの質問をした. とりわけ彼は, どれだけ被害者と親しいかについて知りたがった.

別解 The detective asked the girl many questions. **In particular**, he repeatedly checked with her to find out what time she left the café.

刑事は少女にたくさんの質問をした. とりわけ彼は彼女に何時に喫茶店を出たのか何度も確認した.

7 We had strict rules about how to wear uniforms. **Specifically**, boys were not allowed to wear sweaters under their jackets and girls couldn't wear pantyhose with their skirts.

制服の着方について厳しい規則があった. 例えば, 男子は上着の下にセーターを着ることは認められず, 女子はストッキングをはいてはいけなかった.

別解 We had strict rules about how to wear uniforms. **Specifically**, male students were not allowed to wear their pants below the waistline, and female students couldn't hitch their skirts above their knees.

制服の着方について厳しい規則があった. 例えば, 男子生徒はズボンを腰の位置まで下げてはいけないし, 女性はスカート丈を膝より上にしてはいけない.

8 Some people don't believe the old maxim "honesty pays." **To illustrate**, my boss always says, "If you want to be a good sales representative, you've got to be a liar."

「正直者は得をする」ということわざを信じていない人もいる. 例を挙げるならば, 私の上司はいつも「もし, 優秀な営業になりたければ, 嘘がうまくならなくてはダメだ」といっている.

別解 Some people don't believe the old maxim "honesty pays." **To illustrate**, my husband declares that his motto is "honesty doesn't pay," and, except for me, hardly tells people what he really believes.

「正直者は得をする」ということわざを信じていない人もいる. 例を挙げるならば, 夫は自分のモットーは「正直者はバカをみる」と断言して憚らず, 私以外の人に本音を打ち明けることはほとんどない.

To conclude

結論づける・まとめる

長いエッセイを書く際は，introduction / body / conclusion ということで，最後に conclusion としてまとめを書くのが普通です．しかしライティングでは，多くの英語学習者が最後のパラグラフに書かない方がよいことを conclusion と勘違いして書いてしまうことがあるようです．

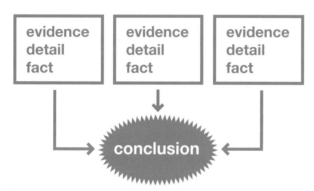

Common expressions

▸ in summary	▸ in brief	▸ to sum up
▸ in short	▸ all in all	▸ to summarize
▸ in conclusion	▸ overall	

Tips to Check 展開は自然に，論理的に

　結論づけたりまとめるためのつなぎ言葉はいくつかありますが，それほどニュアンスに差はありません．それよりも注意しなければいけないのは次の 2 点です．

① 前に述べていないまったく新しいことを書かない

② 最初に述べたこととまったく同じことを書かない．

　さて①ですが，英語のライティングにおいては「衝撃の結末」や「最後のどんでん返し」は要りません．体験を物語的に述べるときでさえ，ストーリーから読み取れる教訓を書くのが普通です．最後に今まで述べていないことを書くのは，長時間議論を重ねた会議

の最後に，偉い人が突然，それまで話していなかった意見を述べて「これにしよう！会議終了！」と言うようなものです。「今までのは何だったんだ」と思うようなまとめは書いてはいけません。

また，矛盾するようですが，②も大事です。最初に述べてきたこと，とりわけ問題提起として「これについて書きますよ」という introduction とほとんど同じ表現でほとんど同じことを書くぐらいならば，conclusion は要りません。introduction と同じならば body を読む必要もないわけですよね。

Exercise

1-3 の各々が論理的に（「結論」として）つながるように，空所を埋めてみましょう。ヒント（💡）に従って，必ず自分なりの解答を作ってみてください。

1

I was in high school until I graduated last year. I currently go to university. This has made me think about how both similar and different the two types of schools are.

The first difference is the clothes students wear. Most Japanese high schools, regardless of whether they are public or private, require students to wear uniforms. This prevents students from expressing themselves through what they wear. In contrast, university students are allowed to wear what they like. Some students, however, may not like this much because they do not want to spend too much time selecting what to wear at the beginning of the day.

Another difference is where students take lessons at school. In high school, students take lessons in the same classroom with the same classmates every day. Each subject's teacher comes in to give a lesson. In contrast, college students have to go to a different classroom for each lesson. Besides, except for some required classes, university students can decide which classes to take. This gives them a lot of independence. However, some students have difficulty finding friends because there is no fixed home room like there was in high school.

Despite the additional freedom and independence that college students have, one thing is the same whether you go to high school or college: students have to study hard. In high school, teachers give students a lot of drills, while in university, students are encouraged to express their opinions and think critically. In either case, students must work hard, both during class time and outside the classroom.

In conclusion, [   ]

[   ]

[   ].

💡 上で述べられた高校と大学の共通点と相違点を短くまとめてみましょう.

2

Gymnastic displays featuring human pyramids are often seen at sport festivals across Japan, from elementary schools to high schools. People often enjoy seeing teams of students forming large pyramids, and teachers like to use this activity to unite their students.

Considering students' safety, however, this activity should be removed from sport festivals' programs. Students in higher places in the pyramid may lose their balance and fall. Additionally, students in lower places have to bear considerable weight. Moreover, many students lack the necessary gymnastic training needed to do the activity safely. In fact, a number of students have become injured due to this activity, and some of them have died.

To sum up, [   ]

```
┌─────────────────────────────────────────────┐
│                                               │
├─────────────────────────────────────────────┤
│                                          .    │
└─────────────────────────────────────────────┘
```

💡 上で述べられた運動会の人間ピラミッド競技の是非とその理由を短くまとめてみましょう.

3

People are often divided into two types. The first type is made up of introverts who are shy and quiet people, and who may not find it easy to talk to others. The second type consists of extroverts who are outgoing and friendly people, and who like being with and talking to others. Let me describe how people in each group behave, as well as their good points and bad points.

Introverts prefer being alone or with people they know. Because of this, they tend to perform well in quiet environments. For example, they are good at reading and writing. They usually outperform extroverts in written reports, which is one important task at schools or in the workplace.

However, they tend to have difficulty working with new people. Therefore, they are not good at participating in discussions at school or work. Even when they have great ideas in their heads, they often miss the chance to express their opinions because they lack excellent oral communication skills.

On the other hand, extroverts perform well when they do their tasks with other people. They do not hesitate to tell their opinions to their peers or colleagues, so they often lead discussions at meetings. They are also good at building relationships with others. They give off good impressions to those around them, such as their coworkers, classmates, bosses, or teachers.

However, some extroverts are not good at solitary tasks. They may not be able to read a lot of the documents necessary to do research or be able to write reports using clear language. In this case, they may need to get help from their coworkers or classmates who are introverts.

All in all,

 人のタイプについて，上記で述べられていることを端的にまとめてみましょう．

完成したら，自分の書いたものと次の Sample Answers をよく比べてみましょう．

── Sample Answers ──

❶

I was in high school until I graduated last year. I currently go to university. This has made me think about how both similar and different the two types of schools are.

The first difference is the clothes students wear. Most Japanese high schools, regardless of whether they are public or private, require students to wear uniforms. This prevents students from expressing themselves through what they wear. In contrast, university students are allowed to wear what they like. Some students, however, may not like this much because they do not want to spend too much time selecting what to wear at the beginning of the day.

Another difference is where students take lessons at school. In high school, students take lessons in the same classroom with the same classmates every day. Each subject's teacher comes in to give a lesson. In contrast, college students have to go to a different classroom for each lesson. Besides, except for some required classes, university students can decide which classes to take. This gives them a lot of independence. However, some students have difficulty finding friends because there is no fixed home room like there was in high school.

Despite the additional freedom and independence that college students have, one thing is the same whether you go to high school or college: students have to study hard. In high school, teachers give students a lot of drills, while in university, students are encouraged to express their opinions and think critically. In either case, students must work hard, both during class time and outside the classroom.

In conclusion, while students are controlled more in high school and given more freedom in college, at both types of schools they are urged to study a lot.

訳　昨年卒業するまで私は高校に通っていた．今は大学に通っている．このことで，私に高校と大学がどのように似ていて違っているかを考えた．

　1つ目の違いは，生徒・学生が着る服である．大部分の日本の高校は公立・私立を問わず，生徒に制服を着させる．このことは，生徒に着ているもので自己表現をする機会を奪う．逆に，大学生は着たいものを着ることが許される．しかしながら，これが好きでない人もいる．というのは，彼らは1日の始まりに何を着るか考えるのに時間をかけたくないのだ．

　もう1つの違いは，学生が学校で授業を受ける場所である．高校では，毎日クラスメイトと同じ教室で授業を受け，それぞれの科目の先生が授業をするために教室に来る．それに対して大学では，学生は講義ごとに違う教室に行かなければならない．それに，必修の授業を除けば，大学生は受ける授業を選ぶことができる．このことは彼らに自由を与える．しかし，高校のホームルームのような固定の場所がないので，友達をつくるのに苦労している学生もいる．

　大学では自由が与えられるにも関わらず，高校に行こうと大学に行こうと，1つの共通することがある．それは，学生は一生懸命勉強しなければならないということだ．高校では，先生は生徒にたくさんの練習問題を出す一方，大学では学生は自分の考えを述べたり，深く考えたりすることが求められる．どちらの場合も，学生は授業中でも教室の外でも一生懸命勉強しないといけない．

　結論として，高校ではより管理され，大学ではより自由があるという違いはあるが，いずれの学校でも，たくさん勉強することが求められる．

2

Gymnastic displays featuring human pyramids are often seen at sport festivals across Japan, from elementary schools to high schools. People often enjoy seeing teams of students forming large pyramids, and teachers like to use this activity to unite their students.

Considering students' safety, however, this activity should be removed from sport festivals' programs. Students in higher places in the pyramid may lose their balance and fall. Additionally, students in lower places have to bear considerable weight. Moreover, many students lack the necessary gymnastic training needed to do the activity safely. In fact, a number of students have become injured due to this activity, and some of them have died.

To sum up, schools should stop adding a human pyramid activity to their sport festival programs. They can find other activities to wow an audience or that can get students to learn to work together.

訳　　日本中の運動会で人間ピラミッドを模した組体操がよく見受けられる. 人々は生徒たちが組になって巨大なピラミッドをつくるのを見て楽しむことが多いし, 教師たちは生徒たちを団結させるためにこの競技を利用するのが好きだ.

しかし, 生徒の安全を考えると, この競技は運動会のプログラムから抹消されるべきである. ピラミッドの高い位置にいる生徒はバランスを失って落ちる可能性もある. 加えて, ピラミッドの低い位置にいる生徒たちはかなりの重さに耐えないといけない. さらに, 生徒の多くはこの競技を安全に行なうのに必要な訓練を受けているわけではない. 事実, この競技で多くの生徒たちがけがをしていて, 命を落とした生徒もいる.

要約すると, 学校は運動会のプログラムから人間ピラミッドを除くべきである. 観客をあっといわせたり, 生徒たちに一緒に取り組むことを学ばせる競技は他にもある.

3

People are often divided into two types. The first type is made up of introverts who are shy and quiet people, and who may not find it easy to talk to others. The second type consists of extroverts who are outgoing and friendly people, and who like being with and talking to others. Let me describe how people in each group behave, as well as their good points and bad points.

Introverts prefer being alone or with people they know. Because of this, they tend to perform well in quiet environments. For example, they are good at reading and writing. They usually outperform extroverts in written reports, which is one important task at schools or in the workplace.

However, they tend to have difficulty working with new people. Therefore, they are not good at participating in discussions at school or work. Even when they have great ideas in their heads, they often miss the chance to express their opinions because they lack excellent oral communication skills.

On the other hand, extroverts perform well when they do their tasks with other people. They do not hesitate to tell their opinions to their peers or colleagues, so they often lead discussions at meetings. They are also good at building relationships with others. They give off good impressions to those around them, such as their coworkers, classmates, bosses, or teachers.

However, some extroverts are not good at solitary tasks. They may not be able to read a lot of the documents necessary to do research or be able to write reports using clear language. In this case, they may need to get help from their coworkers or classmates who are introverts.

All in all, both introverts and extroverts have skills they are good at and those they are poor at, and this affects how they perform at school or work.

訳　人々は2つのタイプに分けることができる. 1つ目のタイプの人々は恥ずかしがりで物静かな内向的な人たちで, 彼らは他人と話すのは苦手なことが多い. もう1つのタイプの人々は明るく気さくな外向的な人々で, この人たちは他人と一緒にいて話をすることが好きである. 各グループの人たちがどのように行動するのかを長所・欠点と共に説明する.

内向的な人はひとりでいることや自分の知っている人たちと一緒にいるのが好きだ. だから, 静かな環境で力を発揮することが多い. 例えば, 読んだり書いたりするのが得意だ. 外向的な人よりも, レポートを書く課題においては勝る. レポートを書くことは学校や職場では重要な課題の一つでもある.

しかし, 彼らは新しい人と一緒に何かをやるのが苦手だ. それゆえに, 学校や会社での議論に加わるのは得意ではない. たとえ頭の中に良い考えがあるときでも, 自分の意見を言う機会を逸してしまうことが多い. 口頭でのコミュニケーション力に長けていないからである.

一方, 外向的な人たちは他人と一緒に課題をこなすときに力を発揮する. 彼らは仲間や同僚に自分の考えを話すことをためらわない. そのため, 会議では議論を率いることも多い. 彼らはまた, 他人と人間関係を築いていくのも得意である. 同僚, 級友, 上司, 先生など周囲の人に自分をよく印象付ける.

しかしながら, 外向的な人には, ひとりでやる課題が苦手な人もいる. 彼らは調べ物をするのにたくさんの書類を読んだりわかりやすい言葉でレポートを書けないこともある. そういう場合は, 内向的な同僚や級友から助けてもらう必要がある.

まとめると, 内向的な人も外向的な人もそれぞれ得意なことと苦手なことがあり, それによって学校や職場でどのように活躍するかが決まる.

強調する

今まで何度も学んできたように，英語では多くの場合，大事なことを最初に述べて，その後補足する，というように展開することがほとんどです．一方で，事実を述べてから，その後強調する表現方法もあります．

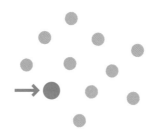

Common expressions

▸ in fact	▸ without a doubt = undoubtedly
▸ indeed	▸ especially
▸ in truth	▸ in particular
▸ truly	▸ above all
▸ certainly	▸ in any event
▸ obviously	▸ of course
▸ clearly	▸ even
▸ absolutely	▸ again

　強調の仕方はいくつかのパターンがあります．よく使われ，且つまずマスターすべき用法は，「事実」「(ところが) 実際のところは」のように前に述べたことの具体例を強調して出す方法です．Section 6 では前に述べたことをサポートする役割としての例の挙げ方を学びましたが，ここでは読み手の意識を具体例に向けます．「一般的にはこう (思われているの) だが実際は」のように前の流れとは違った具体的事実を出すこともあります．会話では actually がよく使われますが，ライティングでは別の表現を使った方がいいでしょう．

 「事実」＋「具体例の強調」

Stress often brings negative effects to workplaces. In fact, people under considerable stress sometimes make horrible mistakes.

ストレスはたびたび職場に負の効果をもたらす. 事実, たくさんのストレスを抱えている人たちは, 時々とんでもない失敗をする.
■ ストレスの負の効果の具体例を強調

Some people are not interested in sports. Indeed, my big sister doesn't play or watch any sport.

スポーツに興味を持たない人もいる. 実際, 姉はスポーツをしないし, 見ることもしない.
■ 姉の興味のなさを強調

Karen received high praise. In truth, she was not happy about it at all.

Karen は大絶賛された. ところが実際のところ, 彼女はそれについて全然喜んでいないのだ.
■ 意外な事実の指摘

前に述べてあることの解釈を述べるときに, 「本当に」「確かに」「間違いなく」というような言葉を使って強調することもあります.

The man finally opened his mouth. What he told us was truly shocking.

男はとうとう口を割った. 彼が私たちに語ったことは本当にショッキングだった.
■ 男が話した内容の解釈

Let's Practice! 解答は p. 117

James Joyce's *Ulysses* won't 　　　　　　　 　　　　　　　 . Certainly, those who don't like complexity and word play find the literary work difficult or boring.

James Joyce の『ユリシーズ』は万人を楽しませる本ではない. 確かに, 複雑な内容や言葉遊びが嫌いな人はこの文学作品を難解や退屈なものと感じるだろう.
■『ユリシーズ』がみんなにとって名著というわけではないという考えを解釈

My wife's face was very red with pinched lips and grinding teeth. Obviously, she 　　　　 　　　　 .

妻の顔は真っ赤で唇は尖っていて, 歯軋りが聞こえる. 明らかに, 彼女は怒っている.
■ 妻の顔の表情を解釈

Jen has lost support from Carla and Missy, and she's running out of money. Clearly, her scheme ☐ ☐ .

Jen は Carla と Missy からの援助も失い，資金が枯渇している．彼女のたくらみは失敗に終わろうとしている．

■ Jen の現況に対しての解釈

....

The millionaire decided to donate a large sum of money to those affected by the disaster. ☐ ☐ ☐ was absolutely wonderful.

その大金持ちは災害に遭った人たちに多額の資金を寄付することにした．彼がしたことはとてもすばらしいことだ．

■ 寄付行動の解釈

....

Joe let me stay at his apartment for more than a few months and helped me get a new job. Without a doubt, he is one ☐ ☐ ☐ a lot.

Joe は数ヶ月もの間，私をアパートに泊めてくれて新しい仕事を見つけるまで援助してくれた．疑いもなく，彼には大きな借りがある．

■ Joe がしてくれたことの解釈

....

前に述べたことの中でも特に重要な場面を強調する方法も学びましょう．

The actress' performance was splendid throughout the movie. Especially, ☐ ☐ ☐ in the last scene captured the viewers' attention.

映画全体を通じてその女優の演技は光っていた．とりわけ，最後の場面での演技は観た人の注意を引いた．

....

The Great East Japan Earthquake in 2011 shocked every person in Japan. In particular, it ☐ ☐ ☐ of people in Fukushima in many ways.

2011 年の東日本大震災は，日本にいた一人一人に衝撃を与えた．とりわけ，この震災はさまざまな形で福島の人たちの生活を変えてしまった．

....

Children should learn ☐ ☐ at school. Above all, they should learn financial management.

子どもは学校で実用的なことを学んだ方がいい．とりわけ，彼らはお金の管理について学んだ方がいい．

It is possible that Emily was seeing somebody other than the victim at that time, but did not want it to be open. In any event, she ⬚ ⬚ ⬚ an alibi for the night.

Emily がその時間被害者以外の誰かと会っていたが，それを秘密にしたということはあり得る．とにかく，彼女はその夜のアリバイを立証することはできなかった．

⊢ in any event は「そういうことがあるにしても事実は」というようなニュアンスです．話し言葉では anyway が使われます．

Our new vice president took all the company's money and disappeared. Of course, the ultimate responsibility rests with our president, ⬚ ⬚ her.

新しい副社長は会社の金をすべて持って失踪した．もちろん，そんな人間を任命した社長の根本的な責任が問われる．

⊢ 当然予想されることを述べるときに使います．

BTS, a Korean male pop idol group, has fans from a wide range of age groups. Even my mother ⬚ ⬚ ⬚ ⬚ ⬚ the group.

韓国の男性アイドルグループ BTS には幅広い年齢層のファンがいる．私の母でさえ，彼らの大ファンである．

⊢ 強調する語の直前に even を置くのが普通です．

I am sorry that I had to miss your event last week. Again, I ⬚ ⬚ ⬚ , but couldn't get out of a client meeting.

先週のイベントに行けなくてごめんなさい．本当に行きたかったのですが，顧客との打ち合わせを抜けられなかったのです．

⊢ この強調の again は必ずしも使いこなす必要はありませんが，英英辞典や英語圏のライティングの教科書でたびたび登場する用法です．

解答

entertain everyone	person I owe	could not provide
was mad	how she acted	who appointed
is failing	changed the lives	is a big fan of
What he did	practical skills	wanted to go

Exercise

1-16 の各々が論理的に（「強調する」展開に注意して）つながるように，空所を埋めてみましょう．必ず自分なりの解答を作ってみてください．

1 Joe and Hailey know each other very well. In fact, ☐
☐.

2 Physics is rarely a girls' favorite subject. Indeed, ☐
☐
☐.

3 Subjects such as philosophy and theater are considered to be useless. In truth, ☐
☐
☐.

4 People's lives have been affected by the introduction of new technology. Among many of the greatest innovations, ☐ truly
☐.

5 The infamous governor did a few good things. Certainly,
☐
☐.

6 What Mr. Sakai told the police doesn't match with his coworkers' testimony. Obviously, ☐.

7 ☐
☐. Clearly, the situation is getting worse.

8 Mr. Browne is planning to sail across the sea in a washbasin. This plan is absolutely ☐.

9 _____.

This type of behavior undoubtedly causes trouble.

10 I learned so many things when I was in high school.

Especially, _____

_____.

11 Some wildlife lives in _____. In particular,

_____ are quite common.

12 Dennis does not like his hometown much. Above all, _____

_____.

13 The young director thought only a certain number of

people concerned about environmental issues could

understand his latest movie's serious theme. In any event,

most people who saw the movie _____

_____.

14 To promote our new product, Jack suggests making a

very unique TV commercial with a movie star and famous

athlete. Of course, _____

_____.

15 Fred worked for five hours without interruption. He even

_____

_____.

16 Nobody has seen the man since Friday. Again, how he

disappeared _____

_____.

完成したら, 自分の書いたものと次ページの Sample Answers をよく比べてみましょう。

❶ Joe and Hailey know each other very well. **In fact**, they lived together in the past.

Joe と Hailey は互いをよく知っている. 実は, 彼らは同棲していたことがある.

別解 Joe and Hailey know each other very well. **In fact**, they went to the same school from elementary to high school.

Joe と Hailey は互いをよく知っている. 実は, 彼らは小学校から高校まで同じ学校に通っていた.

❷ Physics is rarely a girls' favorite subject. **Indeed**, only two female students chose it for their science elective class in my high school.

物理はなかなか女子の好きな科目にはならない. 事実, 私の高校では女子はたった 2 人しか物理を理科の選択科目に選んでいなかった.

別解 Physics is rarely a girls' favorite subject. **Indeed**, my younger sister says she is more interested in earth science or biology.

物理はなかなか女子の好きな科目にはならない. 事実, 妹は地学や生物により興味があると言っている.

❸ Subjects such as philosophy and theater are considered to be useless. **In truth**, these liberal arts have a much longer history as academic subjects than biology or chemistry.

哲学や演劇といった科目は役に立たないと思われている. ところが実際は, これらの人文学は学科として生物学や化学よりもずっと長い歴史がある.

別解 Subjects such as philosophy and theater are considered to be useless. **In truth**, most famous scientists insist that the humanities are as important as natural and social sciences.

哲学や演劇といった科目は役に立たないと思われている. ところが実際は, 大部分の有名な科学者は人文学は自然科学や社会科学と同じぐらい重要だと主張している.

❹ People's lives have been affected by the introduction of new technology. Among many of the greatest innovations, the internet **truly** changed our lifestyles.

人々の生活は新しい技術の導入に影響を受けてきた. すぐれた発明の中でも, インターネットは私たちの生活様式をがらりと変えた.

別解 People's lives have been affected by the introduction of new technology. Among many of the greatest innovations, mobile phones **truly** changed how people communicate with each other.

人々の生活は新しい技術の導入に影響を受けてきた. すぐれた発明の中でも, 携帯電話は, 人々の伝達手段をがらりと変えてしまった.

5 The infamous governor did a few good things. **Certainly**, issuing vouchers for people in poverty helped many people.

悪名高い知事はいくらか良いこともした. 実際, 貧困にあえぐ人々に商品券を発行したことは多くの人々を救った.

別解 The infamous governor did a few good things. **Certainly**, he showed strong leadership at the beginning of this pandemic.

悪名高い知事はいくらか良いこともした. 実際, 彼はこのパンデミックの初期に強いリーダーシップを発揮した.

6 What Mr. Sakai told the police doesn't match with his coworkers' testimony. **Obviously**, he is lying.

Sakai さんが警察に語ったことは, 彼の同僚の証言と矛盾している. 明らかに彼は嘘をついている.

別解 What Mr. Sakai told the police doesn't match with his coworkers' testimony. **Obviously**, One of the two sides is not telling the truth.

Sakai さんが警察に語ったことは, 彼の同僚の証言と矛盾している. 明らかにどちらかが嘘をついているのだ.

7 We lost a lot of clients, and debts have been piling up. **Clearly**, the situation is getting worse.

わが社は顧客を失い, 借金がかさんでいる. 明らかに状況は悪くなっている.

別解 The unemployment rate is at about 20 percent, and prices have spiked. **Clearly**, the situation is getting worse.

失業率は 20%ぐらいあり, 価格は高騰してしまった. 明らかに状況は悪くなっている.

8 Mr. Browne is planning to sail across the sea in a washbasin. This plan is **absolutely** ridiculous.

Browne さんは洗面器で海を横断しようとしている. この計画は本当にばかげている.

別解 Mr. Browne is planning to sail across the sea in a washbasin. This plan is **absolutely** impossible to achieve.

Browne さんは洗面器で海を横断しようとしている. この計画を達成するのは絶対に無理だ.

9 Suzan revealed her supervisor's secret. This type of behavior **undoubtedly** causes trouble.

Suzan は上司の秘密をばらした. こういう振る舞いは間違いなく問題を引き起こす.

別解 Tony is shooting videos of his coworkers to post on social media. This type of behavior **undoubtedly** causes trouble.

Tony は SNS に投稿するために同僚の動画を撮っている. こういう振る舞いは間違いなく問題を引き起こす.

Chapter 1　センテンスを組み立てる

Chapter 2　センテンスをつなげる

Chapter 3　文章をまとめる

⑩ I learned so many things when I was in high school. **Especially**, being a member of the soccer team gave me valuable lessons.

高校の時多くのことを学んだ。とりわけ、サッカー部にいたことが貴重な学びの機会を与えてくれた。

別解 I learned so many things when I was in high school. **Especially**, working as student president helped me acquire leadership skills.

高校の時多くのことを学んだ。とりわけ、生徒会長をやったことはリーダーシップ能力を身につけるのに役立った。

⑪ Some wildlife lives in London. **In particular**, foxes are quite common.

ロンドンには野生動物がいる。とりわけ、キツネはよく見られる。

別解 Some wildlife lives in Tokyo. **In particular**, raccoon dogs are quite common.

東京には野生動物がいる。とりわけ、タヌキはよく見られる。

⑫ Dennis does not like his hometown much. **Above all**, he dislikes hearing people there talk in an unsophisticated manner.

Dennis は自分のふるさとがあまり好きではない。地元の人々の品のないしゃべり方を聞くのは特に嫌だ。

別解 Dennis does not like his hometown much. **Above all**, he does not want to see anybody or anything that bring back unhappy, shameful memories.

Dennis は自分のふるさとがあまり好きではない。とりわけ、彼は嫌な恥ずかしい記憶を思い起こす人や物を目にしたくはないのだ。

⑬ The young director thought only a certain number of people concerned about environmental issues could understand his latest movie's serious theme. **In any event**, most people who saw the movie found it fantastic.

その若い映画監督は、環境問題に関心がある一定数の人たちだけが自分の最新映画の真面目なテーマを理解してくれると思っていた。それとは別に、映画を観たほとんどの人が感動した。

別解 The young director thought only a certain number of people concerned about environmental issues could understand his latest movie's serious theme. **In any event**, most people who saw the movie appreciated its quality.

その若い映画監督は、環境問題に関心がある一定数の人たちだけが自分の最新映画の真面目なテーマを理解してくれると思っていた。それとは別に、映画を観たほとんどの人はその質を高く評価した。

⑭ To promote our new product, Jack suggests making a very unique TV commercial with a movie star and famous athlete. **Of course**, what he suggests is nearly impossible.

新製品の宣伝として，Jack は映画俳優と有名なアスリートが出演するとてもユニークな TV コマーシャルをつくろうと提案した．もちろん，彼の提案はほとんど実現不可能だ．

別解 To promote our new product, Jack suggests making a very unique TV commercial with a movie star and famous athlete. **Of course**, other people disagree with an idea that carries such a huge cost.

新製品の宣伝として，Jack は映画俳優と有名なアスリートが出演するとてもユニークな TV コマーシャルをつくろうと提案した．もちろん，他の人は，そんな多額の費用をかける案には同意しなかった．

⑮ Fred worked for five hours without interruption. He **even** didn't go to the bathroom.

Fred は 5 時間休憩なしで働いた．彼はトイレにも行かなかった．

別解 Fred worked for five hours without interruption. He **even** didn't rise from his seat.

Fred は 5 時間休憩なしで働いた．彼は自分の席から立ちさえしなかった．

⑯ Nobody has seen the man since Friday. **Again**, how he disappeared is exactly the same as the two other cases.

誰も金曜からその男性を見ていない．さて，ここで重要なのは，彼の失踪の仕方は他の 2 つの事件とまったく同じということだ．

別解 Nobody has seen the man since Friday. **Again**, how he disappeared is extremely concerning for this small town.

誰も金曜からその男性を見ていない．さて，ここで重要なのは，彼が姿を消した経緯がこの小さな街では大きな関心事となっている，ということである．

Chapter 1 　センテンスを組み立てる

Chapter 2 　センテンスをつなげる

Chapter 3 　文章をまとめる

To explain or repeat

説明する・繰り返す・言い換える

前に述べたことでは読み手が理解するのに不十分だと思うときは，説明を加えたり，要点を繰り返したり，言い換えたりします.

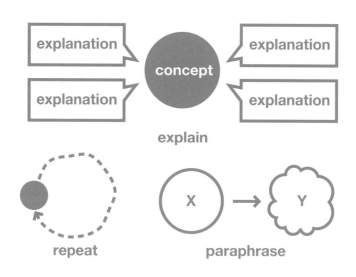

explain

repeat   paraphrase

Common expressions

▸ that is (to say)	▸ in short
▸ to clarify	▸ simply put/stated
▸ to explain	▸ to repeat
▸ in other words	▸ again
▸ to put it differently = to put another way	▸ as mentioned/ explained earlier

　説明・言い換えのためのつなぎ言葉はたくさんありますが，意味にそれほど違いはありません.

Tips to Check 説明・言い換えのつなぎ言葉

Everybody thinks of me as Linda's best friend. That is, they are not interested in what I do.

みんなは私を Linda の親友としか考えていない．つまり，誰も私がすることには関心がないのだ．

The police filed a charge for drunk driving against Ms. Shinohara. To clarify, what she did is against the law.

警察は Shinohara さんを飲酒運転で書類送検した．はっきりさせておくと，彼女のしたことは法律違反だ．

Let's Practice! 解答は次ページ

Government intervention is required. To explain, companies in the industry cannot solve the problem they are facing ⬚　⬚　⬚ the government.

政府の介入が求められている．説明すると，その産業の会社は自分たちが直面している問題を政府からの援助なしには解決できないのだ．

Success is not guaranteed. In other words, you can't always ⬚　⬚　⬚　⬚ .

成功は保証されるものではない．つまり，ほしいものがいつも手に入るとは限らないということだ．

The police have concluded that nobody on the team but Eugene Smith holds a grudge against the coach. To put it differently, Eugene Smith is the ⬚　⬚ .

警察は Eugene Smith 以外の人間はコーチに対して恨みを持っていないと結論づけた．別の言い方をすれば，彼が第一の容疑者だ．

I stepped on a banana peel, fell to the ground, missed my train, was late for the meeting, and made my boss mad. In short, it was ⬚　⬚　⬚ .

私はバナナの皮を踏み，転んでしまい，電車に乗り遅れ，会議に遅刻して上司を怒らせた．手短に言えば，その日はついてなかった．

Heidi was a troublemaker in high school but is now a mayor, while Josh, a then straight-A student, is in jail due to financial misconduct. Simply put, [ ] [ ].

Heidi は高校のときに問題児だったが，今は市長だ．一方，Josh は当時は優等生だったが，財務不正によって留置所にいる．簡単にいうと，人は変わる．

. . . .

Your parents, teachers, and other older people around you may try to offer advice, but what they say rarely helps. To repeat, you should not [ ] [ ] [ ] [ ] about your life or behavior seriously.

両親，教師やその他の周囲の年長者があなたに忠告しようとするかもしれないが，彼らがいうことが役立つことはあまりない．繰り返すが，あなたの人生や行動に関する年長者の言葉をまともに受け入れない方がよい．

➤ 大事な要点を繰り返すときの最も一般的な表現．

. . . .

More and more young people left for the city to find jobs. Again, this is [ ] [ ] [ ].

若い人が，都市に仕事を求めてどんどん出て行くようになった．繰り返すが，これは重大な問題だ．

➤ 直前に述べたことではなくて，以前述べたポイントを振り返るときに使う．

. . . .

As explained earlier, [ ] [ ] financial management skills has more advantages than disadvantages.

前にも述べたように，子どもにお金の管理のやり方を教えることは不利益よりも利点の方が多い．

■ この場合，as explained earlier の直前ではなくて，テキストのずっと前で子どもにお金の使い方を教えることの利点を述べている．

解答

without support from	people change
get what you want	take older people's comments
primary suspect	a major issue
not my day	teaching children

Exercise

1-10 の各々が論理的に（「説明」「繰り返し」「言い換え」の展開で）つながるように，空所を埋めてみましょう．ヒント（💡）に従って，必ず自分なりの解答を作ってみてください．

1 Nobody on the team gave up on the game. That is to say,

_____ .

💡 試合を諦めていなかったということを言い換えればどういうことでしょうか．

2 Robert's violent behavior got his parental authority removed from him. To clarify, _____

_____ .

💡 親権を失うとどうなるでしょう？

3 The two countries made a peace treaty. To explain, _____

_____ .

💡 平和条約を結ぶということはつまり……．

4 Both of the detectives felt that the woman was hiding something. In other words, she _____

_____ .

💡 彼女が隠している事実とは……．

5 Unlike group discussions or oral presentations, tasks that do not require direct interactions do not stop introverts from performing well at school or work. To put it another way, _____ .

💡 内向的な人たちが外向的な人たちより優れている可能性の高いことは？

6 Since Roger saw the beautiful girl for the first time, her existence in his mind grew bigger and bigger until he could not stop thinking about her. In short, _____

_____ .

💡 ひとつの病とも言われるものですね……．

7 [   ]

[   ].

Simply stated, having strict rules does not guarantee better academic performance.

💡 規則を守っている子とよく破る子の比較を述べてみましょう.

8 Kids with poor or neglectful parents won't have any chance to learn how to use money at home. To repeat,

[   ]

[   ].

💡 家庭で教えられないことは, どこで教えるのがよいでしょうか?

9 The girl's parents have disappeared. She is still sixteen, but now she must look after her seven-year-old brother. Again, this is [   ]

[   ].

💡 この事態をどう捉えるべきか書いてみましょう.

10 All the windows were closed, the door was locked, and only the victim had the key. As mentioned earlier, [   ]

[   ]

[   ].

💡 このような状態で問題を解決するにはどうしたらよいでしょうか.

完成したら, 自分の書いたものと次ページの Sample Answers をよく比べてみましょう.

Sample Answers

❶ Nobody on the team gave up on the game. **That is to say**, they believed they could still win.

チームの誰もが試合を諦めていなかった. 言い換えれば, 彼らはまだ自分たちが勝てると信じていたのだ.

❷ Robert's violent behavior got his parental authority removed from him. **To clarify**, Robert is not allowed to see his daughter anymore.

Robert は暴力的な振る舞いをして親権を失った. つまり, Robert はもう娘に会うことができないのだ.

❸ The two countries made a peace treaty. **To explain**, they made an agreement to stop fighting a war.

2ヶ国は平和条約を結んだ. つまり, 戦争をするのをやめる合意をしたのだ.

❹ Both of the detectives felt that the woman was hiding something. **In other words**, she seemed to know where her husband was.

両方の刑事は女性が何かを隠していると感じた. 言い換えれば, 彼女は夫がどこにいるか知っているようなのだ.

❺ Unlike group discussions or oral presentations, tasks that do not require direct interactions do not stop introverts from performing well at school or work. **To put it another way**, introverted people often read and write better than extroverted people.

グループでの議論や口頭発表と違って直接のやりとりを必要としない課題は, 内向的な人たちが学校や職場で活躍する際の障害にはならない. 言い換えれば, 内向的な人は外向的な人よりも読んだり書いたりすることですぐれていることが多い.

❻ Since Roger saw the beautiful girl for the first time, her existence in his mind grew bigger and bigger until he could not stop thinking about her. **In short**, he fell in love with her at first sight.

その美少女を最初に見た時から, Roger の心の中で彼女の存在はどんどん大きくなり, 彼女のことを考えるのをやめることができなくなった. 手短にいえば, 一目惚れしたのだ.

❼ Marika always wears her uniform properly, but her grades are close to the bottom; Sayaka often gets punished for violating the dress code, but gets A's in all her classes. **Simply stated**, having strict rules does not guarantee better academic performance.

Marika はいつも制服をきちんと着ているが, 成績は一番下をさまよっている. Sayaka は服装規定を破り罰を受けることが多いが, すべての授業でA を取る. 簡単にいえば, 厳しい規則は学校のより良い成績を保証しないということだ.

8 Kids with poor or neglectful parents won't have any chance to learn how to use money at home. **To repeat**, <u>financial management skills should be taught at school</u>.

お金がなかったり，子どもをほったらかしにする両親をもつ子どもは，家庭でお金の使い方を学ぶことができない．繰り返すが，お金を管理するスキルは学校で教えた方がいい．

9 The girl's parents have disappeared. She is still sixteen, but now she must look after her seven-year-old brother. **Again**, this is <u>not the kind of situation that allows us to act slowly</u>.

その少女の両親が失踪した．彼女はまだ16歳だが，7歳の弟の面倒を見なくてはならない．考えなければならないことは，これはのんびり構えていていい事態ではない．

10 All the windows were closed, the door was locked, and only the victim had the key. **As mentioned earlier**, <u>we have to discover how the murderer could enter a locked room</u>.

すべての窓が閉まっていて，ドアには鍵がかかっていて，被害者だけが鍵を持っていた．前に述べたように，殺人者がどのようにして密室に入ることができたのか考えなければならない．

時系列・手順を示す

体験を物語風に語ったり，レシピや説明書のように手順を伝えるときの表現方法を学びます．

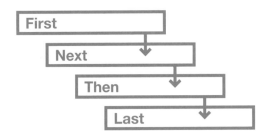

Common expressions

- first, ... second, ... third, ...
- first, ... then, ... next, ... finally, ...
- initially = at first
- previously
- later

- afterwards
- shortly = immediately
- meanwhile
- at that time
- eventually = at last

Tips to Check

　3つや4つ以上の場面を時間軸で述べたり手順を説明する際に，つなぎ言葉を並べる順番を気にするよりも，大事なのは，最初から最後まで流れを止めないような書き方をすることです．

There are a few steps to making a movie. First, write the script. Second, find staff. Third, practice. Finally, film and edit.

映画を創るにはいくつかのステップがある．まず，台本を書く．次に，人員を探す．第3に，練習する．最後に，撮影して編集する．

　このように手順を示すときは，〈つなぎ言葉，＋動詞の原形〉を並べることがよくあります．レシピ，説明書などがそれに当たります．

How I met my husband was not very romantic. First, I worked full-time at a musical instrument store, and he was the owner. I found him to be a nice manager but a terrible salesperson, so I started to lead in sales and the revenue went up. Then, he made me the store manager and left everything to me. He started writing songs and playing the guitar in the back room. He actually had musical talent, and a lot of people came to the store to see him performing. Next, my feelings towards him changed. I still don't know why, but I couldn't stop thinking of him. Finally, I asked him to be my boyfriend, and he agreed. A few months later, we got married.

夫との出会い方はそれほどロマンティックではない．最初，私は楽器店でフルタイムで働いていた．彼はその店のオーナーだった．良い店長とは思ったが，営業力はゼロだった．そこで，営業では私が指揮を執り，売上は伸びた．すると，彼は私を店長に任命して，すべてを任せた．彼は曲を書いて，店の裏でギターを弾き始めた．彼は音楽の才能があり，多くの人が彼が演奏するのを聴くために来店するようになった．その後，私の彼に対する気持ちが変わった．いまでもなぜだかわからないけれど，彼のことを考えるのをやめることができなくなった．とうとう私は彼に交際を申し込み，彼は受け入れた．数ヶ月後，私たちは結婚した．

■ このように出来事・体験を物語的に述べるときには，過去形が基本です．過去においてすでに終わっていたことに〈had ＋ -ed/en 形〉が用いられたり，上の I still don't know why のように話の途中でいまにシフトすることがあれば現在形が使われることがあります．

Let's Practice! 解答は次ページ

At first, ☐☐☐☐☐ ☐☐☐☐☐ well. However, we had a lot of trouble the following year.

最初はすべてがうまくいった．しかしながら，翌年，たくさんの問題が起きた．

Previously, kids were allowed to play in this space. After ☐☐☐ ☐☐☐ ☐☐☐☐☐, though, entering it has been prohibited.

以前は，子どもはここで遊ぶことができた．しかし，事故が起こってから，ここに入るのは禁じられた．

We thought that Jim would be the best and chose him to be our leader. We [　　] [　] [　　　] later.

Jim が最適任だと思い，彼を私たちのリーダーに選んだ．後に，私たちはその判断を後悔した．

Sara and Pete had a big fight over their son's education. Afterward, they [　　] [　　　].

Sara と Pete は息子の教育をめぐって大喧嘩した．後に，2 人は離婚した．

The president announced his resignation. The vice president [　] [　] immediately.

社長は自分の退職を表明した．副社長がすぐに引き継いだ．

Even after Angela got a divorce, Max didn't live with her. Meanwhile, her ex-husband [　　　] a new relationship with his co-worker.

Angela が離婚した後も，Max は彼女と一緒に住むことはしなかった．その間，彼女の元夫は彼の同僚と付き合い始めた．

I was not ready to accept the offer at that time. I [　　] [　] [　] it, though.

私はまだそのときその話を受ける心の準備ができていなかった．しかし，そうすべきだった．
► then と言い換えることもできます．

Police searched for the missing high school student for two weeks. Eventually, she was [　　] to be [　　] in the forest.

警察は，失踪している高校生を 2 週間探した．最終的には，森の中で死体となって発見された．
► 最終的にどうなったのかを述べるときは eventually が最も普通ですが，finally, at last も使えます．

解答

everything worked	took over
an accident happened	started
regretted our decision	should have done
got divorced	found / dead

134

Exercise

1-10 の各々が論理的に（「時系列」「手順」の展開で）つながるように，空所を埋めてみましょう．ヒント（💡）に従って，必ず自分なりの解答を作ってみてください．

1 Here's how to cook curry. [＿＿＿＿＿＿＿＿＿＿], brown the meat. [＿＿＿＿＿＿＿＿＿], add the diced onion to the pot and cook over medium-high heat until it has softened and starts to caramelize on the edges. [＿＿＿＿＿＿＿＿], add potatoes, carrots, and spices. [＿＿＿＿＿＿＿＿], simmer the mixture for at least 20 minutes.

💡〈つなぎ言葉, ＋原型〉を使ってカレーの作り方の説明を完成させましょう．

2 I am currently preparing to go to an acting school in Los Angeles. Here's how I made this decision. First, [＿＿＿＿＿＿＿＿＿＿＿＿＿＿＿＿＿＿＿＿] to become pop queens. Although my friend did not pass, I did. Then, I [＿＿＿＿＿＿＿＿＿＿＿＿＿＿＿＿＿＿]. It was a good experience, but I felt I didn't want to work like this forever. Next, I [＿＿＿＿＿＿＿＿＿＿＿＿＿＿＿＿]. I couldn't act well, but I really had fun creating a story with the other actors. Finally, [＿＿＿＿＿＿＿＿＿＿＿＿＿＿＿＿＿＿].

💡 演劇学校に行くことになった経緯を，順を追って説明してみましょう．

3 Initially, [＿＿＿＿＿＿＿＿＿＿＿＿＿＿]. After I kept practicing for a few months, though, I came to find it entertaining.

💡 続けていたら数ヶ月後に気持ちが変わったことを述べましょう．

4 Previously, [＿＿＿＿＿＿＿＿＿＿＿＿＿＿＿＿＿＿].
After they had an argument over Catherine, however, they have disliked each other since.

💡 何かをきっかけに，2 人の関係が変わったことを説明しましょう．

5 Even when he was in middle school, Chris's guitar techniques were way above anybody else. Later, [_____]

[_____].

💡 子どもの頃にギターがとても得意だった Chris はその後どうなると思いますか?

6 Matthew successfully led a big project. Afterward, [_____]

[_____].

💡 仕事で成功して評価されたので, 立場が変わったことを述べましょう.

7 Mr. Lawrence is out to lunch. [_____] shortly.

💡 今は留守ですが, 昼食が済んだら…….

8 Joe [_____].

Meanwhile, Hailey traveled around the world and enjoyed meeting a lot of people.

💡 Joe は Hailey と対照的な過ごし方をしていたことを述べましょう.

9 Most people were very tired at that time. Therefore, [_____]

[_____].

💡 会議の場がそういう状態だったので, 議長が気をきかせて…….

10 Josh and Patty had an argument many times. Eventually,

[_____].

💡 「雨降って地固まる」 の例を書いてみましょう.

完成したら, 自分の書いたものと次ページの Sample Answers をよく比べてみましょう.

Sample Answers

❶ Here's how to cook curry. **First**, brown the meat. **Second**, add the diced onion to the pot and cook over medium-high heat until it has softened and starts to caramelize on the edges. **Third**, add potatoes, carrots, and spices. **Finally**, simmer the mixture for at least 20 minutes.

これがカレーの作り方です. 最初に, 肉を炒めます. 次に, 鍋に刻んだ玉ねぎを加えて, しんなりと少し焦げ色がつくまで強めの中火にかけます. その後, じゃがいも, にんじん, スパイスを入れます. 最後に, まぜたものを 20 分以上煮込みます.

❷ I am currently preparing to go to an acting school in Los Angeles. Here's how I made this decision. **First**, as a joke my friend and I had an audition to become pop queens. Although my friend did not pass, I did. **Then**, I did a variety of things from singing, to hosting a show, to being a reporter on TV. It was a good experience, but I felt I didn't want to work like this forever. **Next**, I got a role in a TV drama. I couldn't act well, but I really had fun creating a story with the other actors. **Finally**, I found what I wanted to do, and to realize this, I decided to learn acting in the United States.

今私はロスアンジェルスの演劇学校に行く準備をしています. その決心をした経緯はこうです. 最初は冗談で, 友達とアイドルになるためのオーディションを受けました. 友達は通りませんでしたが, 私は受かってしまいました. それから, 歌や, 司会, レポーターなどいろいろなことをやりました. いい経験でしたが, これをずっと続けて行く気にはなりませんでした. 次に, TV ドラマの役をもらいました. 全然うまく演じることはできませんでしたが, 他の俳優さんたちと芝居をするのが本当に楽しかったのです. ついにやりたいことが見つかったので, それを実現するために, アメリカで演技を学ぶことにしました.

❸ **Initially**, I didn't enjoy dancing. **After** I kept practicing for a few months, though, I came to find it entertaining.

最初はダンスが好きではありませんでした. しかし, 数ヶ月練習を続けるうちに, 楽しくなってきました.

❹ **Previously**, Jody and Patrick were good friends. **After** they had an argument over Catherine, however, they have disliked each other since.

以前は, Jody と Patrick は良い友達でした. しかし, Catherine をめぐって言い争いになってからは, 互いに嫌っています.

5 Even when he was in middle school, Chris's guitar techniques were way above anybody else. **Later**, he became a professional guitarist.

中学生の時すでに Chris のギターの腕前は他の誰よりもうまかった。後に，彼はプロのギタリストになった。

6 Matthew successfully led a big project. **Afterward**, he got a promotion.

Matthew は大きなプロジェクトをうまく指揮した。その後，彼は昇進した。

7 Mr. Lawrence is out to lunch. He'll be back **shortly**.

Lawrence は昼食で外出しています。すぐに戻ってくると思います。

8 Joe worked like a bee at the bank. **Meanwhile**, Hailey traveled around the world and enjoyed meeting a lot of people.

Joe は銀行で働き蜂のように働いた。その間，Hailey は世界中を旅して回ってたくさんの人に出会うのを楽しんだ。

9 Most people were very tired **at that time**. Therefore, the chair decided to close the meeting early.

大部分の人々はその時とても疲れていた。それゆえに，議長は会議を早く閉会することにした。

10 Josh and Patty had an argument many times. **Eventually**, they became good friends.

Josh と Patty は何度も言い争いをした。結局は，彼らは良い友達になった。

Chapter 1

センテンスを組み立てる

Chapter 2

センテンスをつなげる

Chapter 3

文章をまとめる

空間配列で描写する

場所や場面を描写するときには空間配列が使われることがあります. 展開する場合には, 一般的にはnear to far (近くから遠くへ), top to bottom (上から下へ), left to right (左から右へ) です.

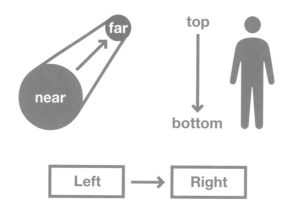

Common expressions

▸ above	▸ between	▸ onto
▸ across	▸ beyond	▸ opposite
▸ against	▸ down	▸ outside
▸ along	▸ in back of	▸ over
▸ around	▸ in front of	▸ through
▸ away	▸ inside	▸ under
▸ behind	▸ next to	▸ up
▸ below	▸ on/to the left/right	
▸ beside	▸ on top of	

空間配列の描写に使われるつなぎ言葉は，場所・位置を表わす前置詞・副詞（に相当する語句）となります．基本的に，あるもの・人と別のもの・人の空間上の位置関係を示すのが描写の基本だからです．

The young man put his hands <u>above</u> his head.

その若い男性は頭に手をやった．

The gas station is <u>across</u> the street.

そのガソリンスタンドは通りを横切ったところにある．

The woman leaned her bike <u>against</u> the fence.

その女性は自転車を塀に立てかけた．

Natalie met her ex-husband by chance when she was walking <u>along</u> the beach.

海岸沿いを散歩していると Natalie は偶然前の夫に会った．

People are gathering <u>around</u> the piano and listening to Akiko's performance.

人々はピアノを囲んで Akiko の演奏を聴いていた．

The man walked <u>away</u> from his wife.

男性は妻のもとを去った． ← 物理的に「離れた」意味にも比喩的に「別れた」という意味にも取れる．

Let's Practice! 解答は p. 144

A woman is working ☐ the counter.

女性はカウンターの後ろで働いている．

....

We live in the apartment ☐ our parents'.

私たちは両親の部屋の下の部屋に住んでいる．

....

The chart ☐ shows the number of Afghan people in Japan.

下のチャートは日本在住のアフガニスタン人の数を表している．

....

A couple of people are selling vegetables ☐ the road.

何人かの人々が道端で野菜を売っている．

Chapter 1 センテンスを組み立てる

Chapter 2 センテンスをつなげる

Chapter 3 文意をまとめる

The new Italian restaurant is [   ] Rob's Café and Beijing Express.

新しいイタリア料理店は Rob's Café と Beijing Express の間にある.

We could see an unusually tall building [   ] the bridge.

橋を越えたところにとてつもなく高い建物があるのが見えた.

John put [   ] his heavy backpack and took a deep breath.

ジョンは重いリュックを下ろして，深い息をついた.

The young lady walked [   ] to the beach.

その若い女性は海岸まで歩いて行った.

Three girls were sitting [   ] [   ] [   ] us.

3人の女の子が私たちの後ろに座っていた.

A politician is giving a speech [   ] [   ] [   ] the station.

政治家が駅の前で演説をしている.

There are still a few people [   ] the building.

まだ何人かが建物の中にいる.

Darin was standing [   ] [   ] his mother.

Darin は母親の脇に立っていた.

A lot of people say the Indian restaurant is pretty good. It is [   ] [   ] the convenience store.

多くの人はその新しいインド料理店はとても良いと言っている. その店はコンビニの隣にある.

The antique store is ☐ ☐ ☐ / ☐ at the end of this street.

そのアンティーク店はこの道の突き当たりの左／右にある.

There was a toaster ☐ ☐ ☐ the refrigerator.

冷蔵庫の上にトースターがある.

Janice climbed ☐ the roof to fix some leaks.

雨漏りを直すために Janice は屋根の上に登った.

Michelle was sitting ☐ Aaron at lunch.

Michelle は Aaron と向かい合って昼食を取っていた.

The detective found the woman standing ☐ the theater.

その探偵はその女性が劇場の外に立っているのに気づいた.

A few kids are playing ☐.

子どもが数人外で遊んでいる.

There is a bridge ☐ the river.

川に橋が架かっている.

Shannon was wearing a sweater ☐ her blouse.

Shannon はブラウスの上にセーターを着ている.

John just walked ☐ the room and left.

John はその部屋を通り過ぎて, 去ってしまった.

There is a fence ☐ ☐ ☐ / ☐ of the house.

家の左／右側には塀がある.

Chapter 1 センテンスを組み立てる

Chapter 2 センテンスをつなげる

Chapter 3 文章をまとめる

The bridge is high enough for a motorboat to go [   ].

その橋はモーターボートが下を通るには十分な高さだ.

My sister is hiding a large amount of money [   ] her bed.

妹はたくさんのお金をベッドの下に隠している.

The schoolboy was running [   ] the stairs to catch the train.

その男子生徒は電車に乗ろうと階段を駆け上がっていた.

The woman heard a strange voice and raised her head [   ].

その女性は変な話し声を聞いたので顔を上げた.

解答

behind	in front of	outside
below	inside	over
below	next to	over
beside	next to	through
between	on the left/right	to the left/right
beyond	on top of	under
down	onto	under
down	opposite	up
in back of	outside	up

Exercise

絵を見ながら，1-24 の各々が論理的に（「空間配列」で描写して）つながるように，
空所を埋めてみましょう． 必ず自分なりの答えを作ってみてください．

1 Irene ⬚ back. A strange man was following ⬚ her.

2 The movie theater won't open until 10:30. ⬚ the theater, however, a few cars are already ⬚.

3 When the high school girl was walking
☐ the street, she saw something
☐ toward her. It was a raccoon dog.

4 Eric was ☐ magic on stage.
☐ him, there were a lot of kids and
parents.

5 The detective [   ] around. Then, he found a small house [   ] the parking lot.

6 My mother has so many comic books [   ] her room. On both sides of the room, bookshelves are [   ] the wall.

7 After [ ] in front of the entrance for a
few minutes, Brian and Jessica went [ ].

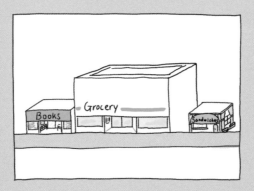

8 [ ] of the grocery store is a small
bookstore. [ ] is a sandwich shop.

9 The [   ] is closed today. In the outdoor dining space, chairs are stacked [   ] each other.

10 Juliette [   ] her boyfriend Romeo on the street [   ] She called [   ] to him.

11 Charlotte _____ the doorbell, but nobody
_____ Then she walked _____ .

12 People are _____ a middle-aged woman.
_____ her, a young, handsome man is
sitting.

13 My parents' house is just a few blocks _____ from the station. _____ the house, there is a small yard.

14 Emily is a pop star, _____ Jen is a talented young actress. _____ the two beautiful women, Jake looked uncomfortable.

15 Ashley is [   ] at a Chinese restaurant.
Her apartment is [   ] the restaurant.

16 Carla [   ] an envelope from a man
wearing sunglasses. [   ] it, there were a
few photographs.

17 Laura _____ the classroom. She was waiting for Mr. Queen _____ in the hallway, though.

18 Michelle and Suzy _____ in the same apartment building. Michelle's apartment is _____ Suzy's.

19 About one hundred meters [ ] the hill, [ ] , was a turn. [ ] was a house shaped like a castle.

20 Charles looked [ ] . A woman with waist-length, chestnut hair was looking [ ] the window.

21 Our car was ⬚⬚⬚⬚⬚⬚⬚ west. The blue sports car was driving off in the ⬚⬚⬚⬚⬚⬚⬚ direction.

22 The old man seemed to know me. He walked ⬚⬚⬚⬚⬚⬚⬚ the floor and sat down ⬚⬚⬚⬚⬚⬚⬚ me.

23 Amy decided to go [ ] the house. She jumped [ ] the fence and fell down [ ] the ground.

24 Bob was [ ] a picture of his ex-girlfriend in his room. When his wife entered the room, he quickly hid it [ ] the table.

完成したら, 自分の書いたものと次ページの Sample Answers をよく比べてみましょう.

┤ Sample Answers ├

❶ Irene <u>looked</u> back. A strange man was following **behind** her.

Irene は後ろを振り返った. 見知らぬ男が後をつけていた.

❷ The movie theater won't open until 10:30. **In front of** the theater, however, a few cars are already <u>parked</u>.

その映画館は 10 時 30 分までは開館しない. しかし, 映画館の前にはすでに車が何台か停まっていた.

❸ When the high school girl was walking **along** the street, she saw something <u>coming</u> **toward** her. It was a raccoon dog.

女子高生が通りを歩いていると, 何かが自分の方に向かってくるのが見えた. それはタヌキだった.

❹ Eric was <u>doing</u> magic on stage. **Around** him, there were a lot of kids and parents.

Eric はステージでマジックをやっていた. 彼を囲むように子どもと親がたくさんいた.

❺ The detective <u>looked</u> **around**. Then, he found a small house **beyond** the parking lot.

刑事はあたりを見回した. その後, 駐車場の向こうに小さな家があるのに気づいた.

❻ My mother has so many comic books <u>in</u> her room. **On both sides** of the room, bookshelves are **against** the wall.

私の母は部屋にたくさんの漫画本をもっている. 部屋の両側とも本棚が壁を埋め尽くしている.

❼ After <u>talking</u> in front of the entrance for a few minutes, Brian and Jessica went **inside**.

2 〜 3 分玄関前で話した後, Brian と Jessica は室内に入った.

❽ **To the left** of the grocery store is a small bookstore. **To the right** is a sandwich shop.

食料品店の左側には小さな本屋がある. 右側にはサンドイッチ屋だ.

❾ The <u>restaurant</u> is closed today. In the outdoor dining space, chairs are stacked **on top of** each other.

そのレストランは今日は閉店だ. 外の食事スペースには, 椅子が重ねて置かれている.

❿ Juliette <u>noticed</u> her boyfriend Romeo on the street **below**. She called **down** to him.

Juliette は恋人の Romeo が下の通りにいるのに気づいた. 彼女は彼のほうに呼びかけた.

Chapter 1　センテンスを組み立てる

Chapter 2　センテンスをつなげる

Chapter 3　文章をまとめる

⑪ Charlotte rang the doorbell, but nobody answered. Then she walked **away**.

Charlotte はドアベルを鳴らしたが，返事はなかった．そこで，彼女は立ち去った．

⑫ People are listening to a middle-aged woman. **Beside** her, a young, handsome man is sitting.

人々は中年女性の話を聴いている．彼女の脇には若いハンサムな男性が座っている．

⑬ My parents' house is just a few blocks **away** from the station. **In back of** the house, there is a small yard.

両親の家は，駅からわずか数ブロックのところにある．家の裏には小さな庭がある．

⑭ Emily is a pop star, and Jen is a talented young actress. **Between** the two beautiful women, Jake looked uncomfortable.

Emily はアイドルで，Jen は才気ある若手女優だ．2 人の美女に挟まれて Jake は居心地が悪そうだった．

⑮ Ashley is working at a Chinese restaurant. Her apartment is **above** the restaurant.

Ashley は中華料理店で働いている．彼女のアパートの部屋はレストランの上にある．

⑯ Carla received an envelope from a man wearing sunglasses. **Inside** it, there were a few photographs.

Carla はサングラスをした男から封筒を受け取った．中には，写真が何枚か入っていた．

⑰ Laura left the classroom. She was waiting for Mr. Queen **outside** in the hallway, though.

Laura は教室を離れた．しかし，彼女は外の廊下で Queen 先生を待っていた．

⑱ Michelle and Suzy live in the same apartment building. Michelle's apartment is **below** Suzy's.

Michelle と Suzy は同じアパートに住んでいる．Michelle の部屋は Suzy の部屋の下だ．

⑲ About one hundred meters **up** the hill, **on the left**, was a turn. **On the right** was a house shaped like a castle.

丘を 100 メートルほど上ると，左手に曲がり角があった．右には城の形をした家があった．

⑳ Charles looked **up**. A woman with waist-length chestnut hair was looking **through** the window.

Charles は上を見た．栗色の髪が腰まである女性が窓から外を見ていた．

㉑ Our car was heading west. The blue sports car was driving off in the **opposite** direction.

私たちの車は西を目指していた．青いスポーツカーが逆方向へ向かっていた．

㉒ The old man seemed to know me. He walked **across** the floor and sat down **next to** me.

その年老いた男は私を知っているようだった．フロアーを横切って歩いてくると，私の隣に腰を下ろした．

㉓ Amy decided to go **inside** the house. She jumped **over** the fence and fell down **onto** the ground.

Amy は家の中に入ることに決めた．フェンスを飛び越えると，地面に倒れた．

㉔ Bob was looking at a picture of his ex-girlfriend in his room. When his wife entered the room, he quickly hid it **under** the table.

Bob は部屋で昔の彼女の写真を見ていた．妻が部屋に入ってくると，とっさにその写真をテーブルの下に隠した．

Chapter 3

文章をまとめる

最後に，IELTS と TOEFL 形式のライティング課題に取り掛かります．

必ず，現在の自分の英語力で書き上げられる答案を作ってみてください．

Sample Answers を参考にしながら，自分の答案で改善できる部分を探し，何度も書き直すことで，一読して内容がパッと頭に入ってくるような論理的な英語が書けるようになってくるはずです．

Section 0
ライティングのプロセスを知る

Chapter 3 では IELTS と TOEFL 形式のライティング課題に実際に取りかかります. これらの試験では文法的に問題がなくても, 全体を通して何が言いたいのかわからない, 内容がスムーズに展開されていない答案は coherence (まとまり) がないとして評価されません. IELTS では coherence and cohesion (まとまりとつながりがあること) が, TOEFL では is well organized and developed (うまく構成され, 展開されていること) が評価されると公式ホームページにはっきり書かれています.

coherence を出すには, 以下の writing process (書く作業をする上で踏むべきステップ) に従ってライティングをすることです. writing process はアメリカでは小学生でも学んでいるようなおなじみの作業です.

1. **Brainstorm** (アイディアをしぼり出す)
2. **Outline** (構成を練る)
3. **Write** (書く)
4. **Revise** (構成・内容を確認して修正する)
5. **Edit** (文法・語彙・スペリング・句読点などを確認し, 修正する)

できれば 2. **Outline** 最低でも 3. **Write** の段階では, 日本語に頼って書くのをやめてください. 英語が苦手な人ほど, 日本語で念入りに下書きをしてそれを英語に訳そうとしますが, 英語と日本語は表現や構成の方法が違います. 自分が書ける英語をうまく組み立てる工夫をするほうが相手に伝わります.

アメリカの小学校の先生は, 2. **Outline** に関して, エッセイやパラグラフの構造をクッキーの OREO に例えて「**O**pinion → **R**eason(s) → **E**xample(s) → **O**pinion again で書きなさい」, あるいは「ハンバーガーのように topic sentence (話題を表わすセンテンス) で始めて, supporting detail (話題をささえる具体例) をいくつかはさんでから, closing sentence (まとめの文) でパラグラフを書きなさい」と教えることがあります. ネイティヴスピーカーも学んでいる型に沿って書いてみるのも 1 つの方法です.

the OREO Strategy

— Opinion
— Reason
— Example(s)
— Opinion (again)

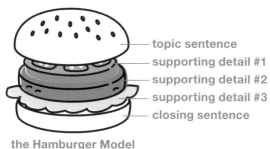

the Hamburger Model

— topic sentence
— supporting detail #1
— supporting detail #2
— supporting detail #3
— closing sentence

　ただし，無理やりこれらの型通りに書こうとして，センテンス間の cohesion（つながり）が悪くなることもあるので注意してください．実際，英検のライティングで「必勝テンプレート」のように扱われることも多い I think that, ... I have three reasons. First, ... Second, ... Third, ... For these reasons, ...（私は…と思う．3 つの理由がある．第 1 に…，第 2 に…，第 3 に…．これらの理由から…）と書くのはやめた方がいいというアメリカ人英語教師もたくさんいます．Chapter 2 の Section 1 から Section 3 で学んだ，Abstract to Concrete, General to Specific, Known to New という原則に従ってさえいれば，1. **Brainstorm** で出した内容に自分が最も合うと考える構成を選ぶほうが的確だと思います．

　もちろん，「文章の構成の仕方は学校などでまったく教えられたことがなかった」「書こうとしてもどういう構成にすればよいのか全く思いつかない」という人もいるでしょう．その場合は，次ページに載せる英文ライティングで使われる典型的な構成を頭に入れておくとよいでしょう．

Intro = Hook + Thesis Statement

- Hook — 自分がこれから述べる話題・問題が読むに値するものである と読み手にアピールする部分
- (Hook の典型 1)These days / Nowadays などで「近頃では〜」と 書く話題への背景を述べる
- (Hook の典型 2) 前置きとして Generally / Some people「一般的 には〜だが」「〜と考える人もいるが」と一般論を述べる
- Thesis statement — 全体を通して言いたいことを述べる

Body

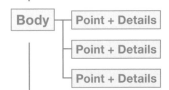

Point + Details

Point + Details

Point + Details

- Point — Thesis Statement の個別の要素. 数や内容は話題による.
- Point と Point の関係は, 列挙する (→ Chapter 2: Section 4), 分類する (→ Chapter 2: Section 5), 定義する (→ Chapter 2: Section 6), 反対意見を述べてから自分の意見を述べる／比較・対 照する (→ Chapter 2: Section 7, Section 8), 因果関係を述べる (→ Chapter 2: Section 9), 問題を述べ, 解決策を示す (problem and solution) などが一般的.
- Detail — Abstract to Concrete / General to Specific / Known to New (→ Chapter 2: Sections 1-3) の原則に従い, それぞれ Point の後にはそれを支える詳細が続く
- (よくある Details の展開) 例を挙げる (→ Chapter 2: Section 10), 説明・強調する (→ Chapter 2: Section 14), 描写する (→ Chapter 2: Section 15) など

Conclusion

- Intro の Thesis statement と Body での各 Point を振り返る. 余計 なことは書かない. (→ Chapter 2: Section 12)
- その他, 適宜, 必要な箇所があれば強調する (→ Chapter 2: Section 11)

3. **Write** でいったん書き上げたら，よく読んで reverse outline（逆構成メモ）を作ってみるのも 4. **Revise** の段階で何をすればわからない人には有効です．自分が書いたすべてのセンテンスに関して Chapter 1 で学んだ Topic ＋ Comment の構造を確認し，Topic が全体を通して自分が書こうとしているテーマに関係していないものを書き直すのもいいでしょう．

最後に，5. **Edit** で形式面の確認をします．文法に関しては，すべての動詞の使い方に注意を払ってください．主語と一致しているか，時制が適切かはもちろん，センテンスの中で正しい使い方をしているかなど気になる点は，*Cobuild Advanced American Dictionary* (Collins) や *Longman Dictionary of Contemporary English* (Pearson), *Oxford Advanced Learner's Dictionary* (Oxford University Press) などの優れた学習英英辞典や『アクシスジーニアス英和辞典』（大修館）や『エースクラウン英和辞典』（三省堂）のような基本語の説明が詳しい辞書で例文と自分の書いたセンテンスを比較するとよいでしょう．実は，この作業をきちんとすれば，ライティングのために初級者・中級者が必要な文法はほとんどマスターできます．目的もなく文法書を通読するよりも効果的です．

正直，自分が書いた英語を読みたくないという学習者は多いでしょう．それほどうまいとは思えない英語を読むよりも，ネイティヴスピーカーやもっと英語が上手い人が書いた英語を読みたいと思うのは自然なことです．でも，ライティング力を伸ばすのは 4. **Revise**, 5. **Edit** をどれだけやれるかにかかっています．

さて，実際にどう Writing Process を行うか，次を見てみましょう．

─ Sample Prompt ─

Some people think that those living 50 years ago were happier than we are now. Do you agree with this statement? Explain your answer with reasons.

50 年前に生きていた人々は，現在の私たちよりも幸せだという人がいる．あなたはこの考えに賛成か．理由を挙げて答えなさい．

1 Brainstorm

「50 年前を生きていた人の方が私たちよりも幸せだ」という考えに同意するかどうかを答え，理由を説明することが課題です．

まずは 50 年前と現在を比べることです．何について比較するかを決めて，次のようにアイディアを出していきます．Brainstorm をすべて英語にする必要はありませんが，ポイントになる表現は書ける限り英語で書いたほうが Outline 以降の作業が楽になります．

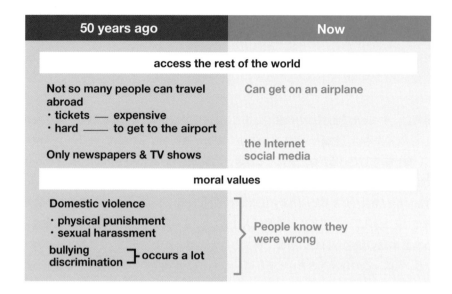

50 years ago	Now
access the rest of the world	
Not so many people can travel abroad ・tickets — expensive ・hard —— to get to the airport	Can get on an airplane
Only newspapers & TV shows	the Internet social media
moral values	
Domestic violence ・physical punishment ・sexual harassment bullying discrimination ⨽ occurs a lot	People know they were wrong

「50 年前が今よりも幸せだ」という考えに同意か反対かがすぐ決まった場合は，次のようなアイディアのふくらませ方も可能です．中央から外側に Abstract to Concrete / General to Specific の原則に開いてどんどん出てくる考えをメモしていきます．

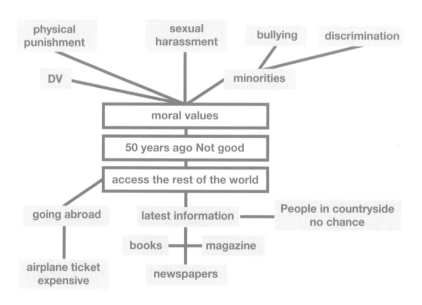

2 **Outline**

書くのに十分なアイディアがたまったら，今度はどのように組み立てるのかを考えます．

■ **Introduction**

Thesis Statement: Life fifty years ago is not as good as life now.

■ **Body**

Point #1—People in the past could not access the rest of the world as people can now.

Detail—Not so many people can get on an airplane

Detail—People in remoted areas cannot know latest fashions or culture

Point #2—People in the past had different values

Detail—In old movies or TV shows:

- Husbands slap wives.
- Teachers punish students physically.
- Men sexually harass women at work.
- Minorities are bullied or discriminated.

■ **Conclusion**

Life is now a lot better than it was fifty years ago.

---

3 **Write**

　実際に書き始めます．決して下書きを日本語で書いて訳したりしないこと．書き終えるまで辞書も使うのはやめておきましょう．

4 **Revise**

　論理・構成面を中心に見直します．

5 **Edit**

　言語面を中心に見直します．

Nowadays, the music, movies, fashion, and food of the 70s are becoming popular again. Some people even say that they want to live in that era—a time when the world was full of energy. However, I don't think that life fifty years ago was as good as is life now.

First, people in the past could not access the rest of the world as easily as they can now. In the 70s, not so many people could get on an airplane and travel abroad. Airplane tickets were fairly expensive, and it took a very long time to even get to the airport. Only rich people in cities had the chance to go to other countries. People living in remote areas had few chances to know the latest fashions or culture. Newspapers and TV shows were their only sources of information. These days, traveling abroad has become more common, everybody can discover what is going on in other countries by using the Internet, and people can even have international friends online.

In addition, people living fifty years ago had different values than we have now. When you watch old TV shows or movies, you may see a lot of surprising scenes. For example, husbands might slap their wives just because they are angry. Classroom teachers might punish students physically. Businessmen might sexually harass their colleagues. Minorities might be bullied or discriminated against in public places. Scenes like these from the movies of the time suggest that such actions regularly occurred in the 70s, but now everybody knows that these are wrong. While all such wrongdoings have yet to be wiped out completely, it is true that people have promoted alternative moral values over the last five decades and thanks to that, fewer and fewer people are unfairly hurt.

In summary, in the past fifty years, the world has gotten closer together and the moral values of society have developed. For these reasons, life is now a lot better than it was fifty years ago.

訳　最近，70 年代の音楽，映画，ファッション，食べ物が再び人気になっている．その時代に生きたいという人さえいる—活気に満ちていた時代に．しかし，50 年前の暮らしが今の暮らしほど良いようには思えない．

第 1 に，過去の人々は今私たちが自分のまわりの世界以外に接するようなことはできないということだ．70 年代では，飛行機に乗って外国旅行をする人はそれほど多くはなかった．飛行機の切符が大変高く，空港に行くだけでものすごい時間がかかっていたからだ．都市に住む裕福な人だけが外国に行くことができた．へんぴな地域に住んでいる人は最新のファッションや文化に触れる機会はほとんどなかった．新聞とテレビだけが彼らの情報源だった．今日では，海外旅行はぐっと身近なものになり，すべての人はインターネットを使って外国で何が起こっているかを知ることができる．そして人々はオンラインで国外の友達をつくることさえできる．

加えて，50 年前に住んでいる人々は今の私たちとは違う価値観を持っている．古いテレビ番組や映画を見れば，びっくりするような場面に出くわすこともあるだろう．例えば，夫が妻を単にむかついたというだけで殴る．学校の先生が体罰と言って生徒を痛めつける．サラリーマンの男性が同僚にセクハラをすることだってある．少数派の人たちが公共の場でいじめられたり，差別を受けたりすることもある．当時の映画にこういう場面があるということは，そのような行いは 70 年代にごく当たり前に起こっていたことが伺えるのだが，現在ではみんなこういうことは間違っていると知っている．このような間違った行いが完全になくなったとは言えないにしても，過去 50 年にわたって新しい倫理観を作り上げてきたことは事実であり，そのおかげで，不当に傷つく人は減ってきている．

要約すれば，過去 50 年にわたって，世界はより身近なものとなり，社会の倫理観は進歩した．これらの理由から，暮らしは 50 年前よりもずっと良くなった．

　　次のページから，IELTS と TOEFL 形式のライティング課題が始まります．次の方法で取りかかるといいでしょう．

1.　**prompt**（お題；課題として問われていること）をよく読んでください．問われていることを勘違いすると当然ながら，いい答案は書けません．

2.　何を書くのか考えて，構成を練ります．〈Brainstorm + Outline〉

3.　実際に書き始めます．決して下書きを日本語で書いて訳したりしないこと．書き終えるまで辞書も使うのはやめておきましょう．〈Write〉

4.　なんとか書き終えたら，見直します．構成面・言語面の両方からよく検討し，必要と感じたら訂正してください．ここでは，辞書やその他の参考書を使って構いません．
〈Revise + Edit #1〉

5.　**Sample Answer** を読みます．一般的な中級程度の英語学習者が到達可能なサンプルにしてあります．IELTS や TOEFL でかなりいい評価を受けるには表現は洗練されていないし，綿密に検討すれば論理はやや甘いところがありますが，論旨は明確ですっと読めるようなものになっているはずです．

6.　自分が作った答案をもう 1 度読み，再び直したいところがあれば修正します．
〈Revise + Edit #2〉

Section 1

2つの意見を検討し 自分の意見も述べる IELTS

Some people think that sports teach kids how to compete, while others think they teach them how to cooperate with other kids.

Discuss both sides and give your opinion.

Write at least 250 words

スポーツは子どもに競争の仕方を教えるものだと考える人もいれば，他の子どもと協力する方法を教えるものだと考える人もいる.

両方の意見について議論し，あなたの意見を述べなさい.

Intro

- 与えられた prompt を自分の言葉で言い換える.
- あるいは, 何について書くのかを簡潔に述べる.
- ここでは「子どもはスポーツから多くを学ぶ」ことを書き, 多くは何かと読み手に考えさせる.

Opposite opinion

- 「両方の意見を論ぜよ」と指定してあるので, まずは自分が主張したい意見と反対の意見を述べる.
- 子どもがスポーツで競争することを学ぶと述べ, Abstract to Concrete の原則に従って, 説明する.

Opinion

- パラグラフの最初で, 「これだけではない」と述べて, 読み手に自分が本当に伝えたい意見はこちらだと理解させる.
- その上で, 「子どもは協力することをスポーツから学ぶ」と述べ, それを説明する. ここでも Abstract to Concrete / General to Specific の原則に従う.

Conclusion

- まとめ. 余計なことは書かず, 第2, 第3パラグラフの要約につとめる.

Children learn many things. While it is true that they gain a wide range of knowledge at school, from math and history to science and literature, they also learn some important skills through sports.

People naturally compare themselves with others. This also applies to children playing sports. When other kids perform better than them, they feel envy or unhappiness. Likewise, when they outperform others, they feel good. These feelings motivate them to improve their performance. Like any academic subject, successful kids compare their performance with that of other people to grow their strengths and overcome their weaknesses.

This is not the only thing children can learn from sports. They also learn how to work with others. When they play on a team, they inevitably work together to win. For example, when I was on the soccer team in high school, I had to tell what I had in mind to my teammates, while also listening to their opinions, for us to perform better as a team. Teamwork is even built when you practice an individual sport, such as tennis and swimming. Like in academic subjects, students who do sports share problems and ask questions of each other to perform better. Kids do not always focus on outperforming others. They also think about offering help and solving problems as a team.

As regular classes do at school, sports give children opportunities to learn how to cooperate as well as how to compete. It is nice to help children have such opportunities.

❗ ここがポイント

People naturally compare themselves with others. **This** also applies to children playing sports. When other kids perform better than them, they feel envy or unhappiness. Likewise, when they outperform others, they feel good. These feelings motivate them to improve their performance. Like any academic subject, successful kids compare their performance with that of other people to grow their strengths and overcome their weaknesses. **This** is not only the thing children can learn from sports.

☞ Sample Answer では 2 ヶ所で This がセンテンスの頭で使われています. 第 2 パラグラフの This は前にでてきたもの・ことではなく, 前のセンテンスの内容全般を受けています. 第 3 パラグラフの最初のセンテンスの頭の This は第 2 パラグラフ全体を指しています. このような, 前の内容とつなげる重要な This を使えるようになるとライティング力はぐんと伸びます.

訳 子どもはたくさんのことを学ぶ. 数学や歴史や理科や文学などたくさんの知識を得るのはもちろんだが, スポーツを通じて重要なスキルを身につけもする.

人間は生まれながらにして自分と他人を比べてしまう. このことはスポーツをする子どもたちにもあてはまる. 他の子どもが自分よりもうまいと, うらやんだり不満に感じたりする. 同じように, 自分が相手よりもうまくいっていると気分が良くなる. これらの感情は子どもたちにうまくなろうという気にさせる. 学校の教科と同じように, できる子は自分のプレイと他の子どものプレイと比べて, 自分の長所を伸ばして, 弱点を克服する.

子どもがスポーツから学ぶのはこれだけではない. 彼らはまた他人と一緒にやるということを学ぶ. チームスポーツをすると, 必然的に勝つために一緒にやる. 例えば, 私は高校時代にサッカー部に入っていたが, 勝つためには, チームメイトに自分が考えていることを伝えたり, チームメイトの考えを聞く必要があった. チームワークはテニスや水泳のような個人競技をするときにさえ, 磨かれる. 学校の教科と同じように, スポーツをする生徒は問題を共有したり, 質問し合うことでうまくなろうとする. 子どもはいつも相手を出し抜くことばかりに気をとられているのではない. 彼らは救いの手を差し伸べたり, チームで問題解決することに頭を使うこともあるのだ.

スポーツは, 通常の授業と同様に, 子どもに競争だけでなく協力することを学ぶ機会を与える. 子どもにそういう機会を与えるのは良いことだ.

Section 2

与えられたテーマの是非を検討する IELTS

Some celebrities, such as pop music icons, movie stars, and famous athletes, often share their views on public issues that are not relevant to their specialties.

Is this a positive or negative development?

Write at least 250 words

大衆音楽の象徴的存在，映画スター，有名スポーツ選手などの有名人の中には，自分の専門分野とは関係のない社会問題について，度々自身の見解を述べる人がいる.

この兆候は肯定的に捉えられるべきか，それとも否定的に捉えられるべきか.

Intro

- 与えられた prompt を自分の言葉で言い換える.
- 文脈・状況とともに問題設定をする.
- 賛成か反対か自分の立場を明らかにする.

Reason #1

- 良いと考えられる点として「自由に意見を述べるようになったこと」を挙げる.
- そう述べたからには, 以前は「自由に意見を述べることはできなかった」ということになるので, 過去の有名人の発言がどのように扱われてきたかを説明する.

Reason #2

- 第2の理由を挙げる. 可能ならば, 完全に並列で2つの理由を並べるよりも, 第1の理由から発展したものが望ましい. ここでは,「有名人のコメントから, ごく普通の大衆の意見が受け入れられる」ことを挙げる.
- 「大衆の意見＝正しい」とは限らないので, そのことを認めた上で, 有名人の発言が, 専門家と大衆の考えの乖離に気づきを与える機会になることを指摘する.

Conclusion

- 余計なことは書かず, ピリオド代わりに簡潔にまとめる.

More and more celebrities express their honest opinions regarding public issues on social media such as Instagram, Facebook, and X (formerly knowns as Twitter). For example, Taylor Swift, a popular American singer, made a comment on her social media account after a terrible school shooting occurred in Texas. There may be some criticism that such comments are outside a celebrity's specialty and may mislead people, but I consider this trend to be positive.

First, it is good that celebrities have found a way to express themselves freely and that their fans can access it. Before social media appeared, celebrities' comments were filtered. Media often reported only the parts they thought were worthy. Sometimes what they said was quoted out of context, and they received unfair criticism. Putting what they think on social media shifts the responsibility for delivering messages to the celebrities themselves, so they are misinterpreted less often.

In addition, through celebrities' comments, the general public's reactions to public issues are widely shared. It is true that celebrities are not specialists in most public issues, but this also means that they share the same concerns as the public about them. These types of opinions are often ignored, and people in power often lack the ability to know how ordinary people feel about policies made based on specialists' advice. Celebrities' comments can help decision makers become aware of the general public's opinions on public issues.

Despite a few negative points, overall, it is a good thing that celebrities have become able to comment on public issues.

■ ここがポイント

There may be some criticism **that** such comments are outside a celebrity's specialty and may mislead people, but I consider this trend to be positive.

It is true that celebrities are not specialists in most public issues, **but** this also means that they share the same concerns as the public about them.

☞ライティングで自分の意見を述べるときに，自分の意見とそれが正しいと思う理由をひたすらグイグイと書き連ねるとうまくいかないことがあります．とくに，明らかに意見が分かれるような問題に関して一方的に自分の主張だけを押し通そうとすると，ひとりよがりの幼稚な意見のように響くことさえあります．それを避けるためには，Sample Answer にあるような反対側の意見を述べて，自分が幅広い視点から問題を考えていることをアピールするのが有効です．

訳 有名人が Instagram, Facebook, X（旧 Twitter）といった SNS 上で社会問題に関する率直な意見をどんどん述べるようになってきている．例えば，Taylor Swift というアメリカの有名歌手はテキサス州で起こった恐ろしい学校銃撃事件の後に SNS に意見を載せた．こういう発言は専門外であり，人々を誤った方向に導く可能性があるという批判はあるだろうが，私はこの傾向を肯定的に捉えている．

第一に，有名人が自分の意見を自由に述べる場を見つけ，ファンが彼らの意見にアクセスできるということは良いことである．SNS が登場する前は，有名人の発言はふるいにかけられていた．メディアは自分たちが価値あると考える部分だけを報道した．ときには，彼らの発言は文脈を無視して取り上げられて，不当な批判にさらされることもあった．SNS に自分の考えを発表するということは，メッセージを発信する責任を有名人自身が負うことになるので，彼らが誤解を受ける危険性は少なくなる．

加えて，有名人の発言を通じて，公共の問題に関しての一般大衆の反応が広く共有されるようになる．みんなが話題にするほとんどの問題においては有名人は専門家ではないというのは事実だが，このことは同時に彼らはそういう問題に関する大衆と同じ関心を共有しているということでもある．この種の意見はよく無視され，権力についている人たちは，専門家の見解に基づいてなされた政策についてごく普通の人がどう感じているかを知る能力に欠けることが多い．有名人の発言は，政策決定者が公共の問題についての一般大衆の考えを認識するのに役立つ．

いくつかの否定的な要素はあるものの，全体的には，有名人が公共の問題に関して発言ができるようになったのは良いことである．

Section 3 原因を分析して改善案を提示する IELTS

Some students today have difficulty concentrating or paying attention at school.

What are the reasons for this?
What can be done to solve this problem?

Write at least 250 words.

最近，学校での集中力や注意力が低下している生徒がいる.

その理由は何か.

この問題を解決するためにはどうしたらよいか.

Intro

- 与えられた prompt を自分の言葉で言い換える.
- 問題とその背景を説明する.
- 以下に問題の原因および解決策を述べることを示す.

Problem

- 問題の原因を述べる.
- ここでは注意を惹きつけるものが周りに多すぎること, すぐに終わらせなければいけない作業が多すぎることを説明する.

Solution

- 原因にあった解決策を示す.
- 最初の原因である「注意を惹きつけるもの」を一時的に断つことを 1 つめの解決策とする.
- 第 2 の原因である「すぐ終わらせなければいけない作業」とは反対の「時間をかけてゆっくり取り組む」ことの大切さを解く.

Conclusion

- まとめ. 余計なことは書かず, 第 2, 第 3 パラグラフの要約につとめる.

These days educators and psychologists repeatedly point out that the attention span of school children has become shorter. Students go to school to study, but if they cannot keep their concentration for even one class period, it is a serious problem. What has caused this and how can it be fixed?

Obviously, one cause for today's students' short attention span is that there are so many eye-catchy things surrounding them. When they text their friends, they use a variety of fancy emoji. In short video clips they watch in their free time, there are so many things to turn their heads. On top of that, at workplaces, at schools, or in any other place, people are expected to get things done or achieve results quickly. Given any of these reasons, some children have unconsciously lost their ability to stay attentive.

To get such children back to normal, what should be done is surprisingly simple. Children with a short attention span should be kept away from anything eye-catchy, from social media or video streaming services to text messaging apps, for a while. Instead, they should be given tasks to work on little by little without tight deadlines. These types of tasks include reading whole novels or doing research on a particular theme throughout the term. These not only help them improve their attention spans but also foster creativity and develop critical thinking skills.

Children who cannot pay attention at school should be kept away from anything flashy for a period of time and engage in some activities that help them use their imagination and thinking skills.

! ここがポイント

To get such children back to normal, what should be done is surprisingly simple. Children with a short attention span should be kept away from anything eye-catchy, from social media or video streaming services to text messaging apps, for a while. Instead, they should be given tasks to work on little by little without tight deadlines.

Children who cannot pay attention at school should be kept away from anything flashy for a period of time and engage in activities that help them use their imagination and thinking skills.

☞ Sample Answer では何度か should が意見を述べるときに使われています。慣れない学習者は should だけでなく，I think (that) … should としてしまいがちですが，意見を述べるときにそれが書き手の意見なのは当たり前なので，I think (that) … は不要です。

訳 近頃，教育学者や心理学者は子どもの注意力が長く続かなくなっているのを何度も指摘している。生徒たちは勉強をするために学校に行っても，1時限の間でさえ集中力を保つことができないのであれば，これは深刻な問題だ。この原因は何で，どのように改善することができるだろうか。

明らかに，今日の生徒の注意力が持続しない原因は，彼らの周りにたくさん目を惹くものがあることだ。友達とチャットするときには，さまざまな種類の奇抜な絵文字がある。ひまなときに見る動画には，注意を惹くものがたくさん入っている。加えて，職場でも学校でも，他のどの場所においても，人々はすぐに終わらせて結果を出すことが求められている。こういった理由から，子どもは意識しないうちに集中力を失っている。

これらの子どもたちを正常な状態に戻すためにしなければいけないことはごく簡単だ。集中力が続かない子どもは SNS や動画視聴サービスからチャットアプリに至るまで目を惹くものから，しばらくの間遠ざけておくとよい。代わりに，彼らはきつい締切なく少しずつ取り組む課題を与えられるとよい。どういう課題かといえば，学期にわたって小説をまるごと読むことや，決められたテーマを調べたりすることなどだ。これらは集中力を持続させるのに役立つだけでなく，想像力を育み，クリティカルシンキングの技術を伸ばす。

学校で集中することができない子どもたちは一定期間目を惹くものから遠ざけて，想像力や思考力を使う作業にとりかからせるべきである。

Agree or disagree and provide reasons

賛成／反対意見と
その理由を述べる　IELTS

Advice from older to younger people about how
they should live and behave is not helpful to
young people and their futures.

To what extent do you agree or disagree?

Write at least 250 words.

年配の人から若い人への，生き方やふるまいに関するアドバイスは，若者と彼らの将来にとっ
て役に立たないものである．
あなたはどの程度賛成か，あるいは反対か．

Intro

- 与えられた prompt に少し状況を足しつつ自分の言葉で言い換える.
- どの程度賛成あるいは反対なのか自分の立場を明らかにする.

Reason #1

- 役に立たないと考えられる理由として「相手のことを思ってアドバイスをしているわけではない」ということを挙げる.
- 挙げた理由の説明「相手のことを思っていないのであれば, なぜ年配の人は若者に話をするのか」→ 若者と話したいだけ.
- 具体例を挙げる.

Reason #2

- 第 2 の理由として「時代の変化」を挙げる.
- 「どう変わっていったのか」「それがアドバイスが役に立たないことにどう影響するのか」を例を挙げながら説明する.

Conclusion

- 余計なことは書かず, 上に挙げた 2 つの理由を少し違う表現を使いながらまとめる.

Some older people tend to give advice to younger people about their lifestyles or behaviors. Except for very rare cases, though, this type of advice does not seem to help young people. There are a few reasons for this.

First, in most cases, few older people give advice to young people with the actual intention of helping them. Instead, they usually want to look for people to talk with them, or they want somebody to listen to what they did in the past and admire them. I used to have a boyfriend ten years older than me. He liked to talk about how much effort he made when he was about my age. When I asked him for practical advice, he didn't tell me anything concrete. Thinking back on it now, I think that he just wanted to talk with me and impress me. I don't have any complaints about the past relationship with him, but this made me realize that you can't ask for older people's advice.

Another reason why advice from older people rarely works is that things have changed a lot since they were young. For example, when my parents were about my age, the economy was extremely good, and most high school graduates were able to get jobs without any effort. Now, however, we are in a depression. They blamed me for not being able to get a job after I graduated from college. During that period, I desperately wanted a job and went to a lot of job interviews in vain, but I couldn't get any. I know they were just worried about me, but their words, made without knowing the current job market, often hurt me. Additionally, when talking with them, I think their ideas about social issues are out of date, and their lack of awareness about issues such as diversity or sustainable energy often disappoints me.

There might be some exceptions, but basically, I don't take older people's advice about my life or behavior seriously because they usually want to talk about themselves, and they hardly know how things are now.

▐▌ ここがポイント

☞「小論文や英語のエッセイは感想文ではないのだから，個人的な感想を書いてはいけない」という英文ライティングでのアドバイスを受けたという学習者はいるようですが，今回の Sample Answer では第1の理由に「元カレ」を，第2の理由に「両親」という個人的な体験を具体例に使っています．結論から言えば，ほとんど満点に近いような答案を作るというのでもない限り，自分の体験を具体例に使っても問題はありません．ただし，自分の意見を支えるための具体例として誰が読んでも適切なものであり，Abstract to Concrete, General to Specific という大原則に沿って論理がきちんと展開されている必要があります．

訳 年配の人の中には若い人に生活スタイルや立ちふるまいについて説教をする人もいる．しかし，ごくまれな場合を除いては，この種の説教は若者の役には立たないように思える．これにはいくつかの理由がある．

第一に，ほとんどの場合において，本気で若者の力になりたいと思ってアドバイスをする年配の人はわずかだからである．そうではなく，彼らは大概，話し相手を探しているか，誰かに自分が過去にしたことを聞いてすごいと思ってほしいのである．私は以前10歳歳の離れた彼氏がいた．彼は自分が私ぐらいの年齢のときにいかに努力をしたかを話すのが好きだった．私は彼に実際に役に立つアドバイスを求めたときに，何ひとつ具体的なことは言ってくれなかった．今振り返れば，彼はただ私と話をして，感心させたかっただけだったのだと思う．彼との過去の関係に文句を言うつもりはないが，このことで歳上の人にアドバイスを求めてはいけないのだとよくわかった．

年配の人からのアドバイスがうまくいかない他の理由は，彼らが若者の時から世の中はすっかり変わってしまったということである．たとえば，私の両親が私の歳のころは，景気はものすごく良くて，ほとんどの高卒の若者は何の苦労もなく仕事が見つかったのだ．しかし，今は私たちは大不況のさなかだ．両親は私が大学卒業後に仕事を見つけられないことで私を責めた．そのとき，私自身仕事を見つけたくてたまらず，あてもなくいくつもの就職面接に行ったのだが，ひとつも通らなかった．彼らはただ私のことを心配していただけとは今はわかるのだが，現在の就職市場がわかっていない彼らの言葉には，傷つくこともたびたびだった．加えて，彼らと話しているとき，社会問題についての彼らの考え方が時代遅れで，多様化や持続可能なエネルギーについての認識がないことにがっかりすることがよくある．

例外はあるだろうが，基本的には，私は年配の人の人生や行動に関するアドバイスは真に受けないようにしている．彼らはたいてい自分語りをしたいだけであり，ほとんど今の世の中をわかっていないからだ．

Support your opinion with reasons and examples

意見を裏付ける理由と
例を挙げる TOEFL

Directions:

Read the question below. You have 30 minutes to plan, write, and revise your essay. Typically, an effective response will contain a minimum of 300 words.

以下の質問を読んで小論文を書きなさい. 構成を考え, 文章を書いて修正する時間は 30 分です. 通常, 効果的な回答は 300 ワード以上です.

Question:

Some high schools require all students to wear school uniforms. Other high schools permit students to decide what to wear to school.

Which of these two school policies do you think is better? Use specific reasons and examples to support your opinion.

すべての生徒に制服の着用を義務付けている高校もあれば, 生徒が何を着て学校に行くかを決めることを認めている学校もある.
これら 2 つの学校の方針のうち, どちらがよりよいと思うか. 具体的な理由と例を挙げて自分の意見を裏付けなさい.

Intro

- 与えられた prompt を自分の言葉で言い換える.
- 賛成あるいは反対なのか自分の立場を明らかにする.

Reason #1

- 賛成側の理由である「制服を着ることが経済的に良い」ということに反論する.
- 「維持費を考えると決して安くはない」ということを具体例を挙げながら説明する.

Reason #2

- 第 2 の理由として賛成側がよく主張する「勉学に集中できる」を論駁する.
- 生徒側は規則をいかに潜り抜けるか,教師側は生徒が規則を守っているかを監視するのにエネルギーを使い,かえって勉強に集中できなくなっているということを指摘する.
- 具体例を挙げる.

Conclusion

- 余計なことは書かず,上に挙げた 2 つの理由を少し違う表現を使いながらまとめる.

Some adults insist that imposing a uniform policy on high school students is a good idea. They say that students would not have to worry about what to wear every morning and could focus on studying. They also mention that, thanks to uniforms, parents would not have to buy a lot of clothes for their kids. Are these true? Do uniforms truly benefit students? According to my experience, I can't answer yes to these questions.

First, uniforms rarely save parents financially as the supporters of uniform policies insist. A uniform is pretty expensive, and low-income families may find it difficult to purchase one for their kids. In addition, uniforms are not comfortable to wear for long hours, and most students change clothes after they get back home from school. Plus, uniforms often need extra care to look neat. They need ironing and dry cleaning regularly. Just to save time and money, there are a lot more comfortable clothes. Isn't it better for students to wear T-shirts and jeans? Or on cold days, they could wear hoodies or sweatshirts on top.

I also disagree with the idea that uniforms help students concentrate on studying. I even think that uniforms distract the attention of students and teachers. Schools with uniforms have strict sets of rules about how to wear them, but students often break these rules. Male students loosen their ties, untuck their shirts, or wear their pants below the waistline, while female students hitch their skirts way above their knees. However, teachers keep an eye on students and check whether they wear their uniforms in the right way. When I was in high school, teachers holding rulers checked how short my skirt was and asked me to lower it on the spot if they thought it was too short. I often felt uncomfortable during these checks by teachers. Wasn't it just sexual harassment? In fact, one teacher who talked honestly with us complained, "I didn't want to be occupied watching over my students. Instead, I would like to develop my content knowledge and teaching skills." I don't know how many other teachers felt the same way, but some seemed to enjoy putting us under their control. What is true, however, is that teachers don't have to spend time monitoring students and students don't have to be bothered by their teachers' surveillance if there isn't a uniform policy.

To conclude, a uniform policy is not cost-effective or timesaving. Therefore, students should be allowed to wear clothes comfortable to them. This probably will have a more positive effect on their studying.

!■ ここがポイント

☞ 制服の是非は，高校の教科書や入試の自由英作文などでも頻出トピックです．ベタな構成と出尽くした意見による凡庸すぎる答案になりがちです．Sample Answer では「賛成派の大人たちはこういうけれども，実際制服を着る当事者としては」という視点から書くことで，読み手に訴える工夫をしています．

訳 制服規定を高校生に課すのは良い考えだと主張する大人もいる．彼らによると，生徒たちは朝何を着るのか頭を悩まされなくてよくて，勉強に集中できる．また，制服のおかげで両親はたくさんの服を自分の子どもに買わなくて済む．これらは本当だろうか？制服は本当に生徒にとってメリットがあるのだろうか．私の経験からすると，これらの質問に「はい」とは答えられないのだ．

まず，制服があったほうがいいという人が主張するように制服が両親を経済的に救うということはまずない．制服一式はかなり高く，収入の少ない家庭が子どものために購入するのは大変だ．加えて，制服は長時間着るには快適なものではなく，たいていの生徒は帰宅後すぐに着替える．さらに，制服はきちんとした状態にするには余分な手間が必要になる．定期的にアイロンをかけたり，ドライクリーニングに出したりしないといけない．単に時間とお金を節約するためだけなら，もっと快適な服はある．T シャツとジーンズではダメなのだろうか？寒い日は上にバーカーやトレーナーを着ればよい．

制服があると生徒が勉強に集中できるという考えにも賛成しない．制服は生徒や先生の注意を散漫にさせるとさえ私は思う．制服のある学校は着方について厳しい規則があるが，生徒はこれらの規則をよく破る．男子生徒はネクタイをゆるめ，シャツの裾を外に出し，ズボンは腰ばきをするし，女子生徒はスカート丈をひざよりずっと上まで短くする．その一方，教師は生徒を監視し，彼らが正しく制服を着ているのかを検査する．私が高校生のとき，先生たちは定規をもって私のスカート丈の長さを測り，短すぎると丈を下ろすように命じた．先生にこういう検査をされている間，気分が悪くなることがあった．これはまさしくセクシュアルハラスメントではないだろうか．実際，本音で話してくれる先生はこう文句を言っていた．「生徒を監視することばっかり気をとられていたくなんかないんだ．それよりも教科の知識や教える技術を伸ばしたいんだ」私は他の先生のうち何人が同じように感じていたのかわからないが，私たちを自分の支配下におくのを楽しんでいる先生もいた．言えることは，もし，制服がなければ，先生は生徒の監視に時間を使う必要はないし，生徒たちは先生からの監視に悩まされることもないのだ．

結論として，制服指定は費用の面でも時間的にも効率的とは言えない．だから，生徒は着たい服を着れるようになっていたほうがいい．このことは，おそらく彼らの学習面にプラスの効果を生むだろう．

Chapter 1 センテンスを組み立てる

Chapter 2 センテンスをつなげる

Chapter 3 文章をまとめる

Section 6

具体的な理由や 例を挙げる [TOEFL]

Directions:

Read the question below. You have 30 minutes to plan, write, and revise your essay. Typically, an effective response will contain a minimum of 300 words.

以下の質問を読んで小論文を書きなさい. 構成を考え, 文章を書いて修正する時間は 30 分です. 通常, 効果的な回答は 300 ワード以上です.

Question:

Describe a custom from your country that you would like people from other countries to adopt.

Explain your choice, using specific reasons and examples.

あなたの国の慣習 (古くからのならわし) の中で, 他の国でも取り入れてもらいたいものを 1 つ選んで説明しなさい.
選んだならわしについて, それを選んだ具体的な理由と例を挙げて説明しなさい.

Intro

- custom について簡潔に書くことで読み手をテーマに引きずり込む.
- 他国に定着させたい自国の custom を挙げる.

Opposite opinion

- 西欧では銀行や商店・オフィスなどと同様に, 家庭内でも靴を脱がないことが普通ということを述べる.

Reason #1

- 靴を室内では脱ぐことで血行が良くなるという健康上の理由を挙げる.
- より具体的に説明する.

Reason #2

- 第2の理由として床があまり汚れないという衛生面の理由を挙げる.
- 人がカーペット上に座ったり, 寝転がったりすることなど, 具体例を挙げながら説明する.

Conclusion

- 日本が清潔だと言われることに触れながら, 室内では靴を脱ぐべきという自分の意見を繰り返す.

Each community has different customs or conventions, and most of them have survived based on each place's needs. Therefore, it is not easy to import them to other communities. To illustrate, people in cold areas probably can't practice most of the customs created in warm areas—it is impossible for people in Denmark or Finland to wear Hawaiian shirts throughout the year. That said, I would like one custom in Japan, where I was born and grew up, to prevail in other counties: taking off shoes before entering a house.

Many people in Western countries wear shoes inside their houses. For them, doing so might seem as natural as we feel it is to wear shoes in buildings such as stores, banks, or other offices. Even so, I think it is better to practice the custom of not having shoes on inside homes.

One reason why not wearing shoes at home is better is that our feet should not be under pressure for long hours. When wearing shoes, feet are squeezed into tight spaces, which results in poorer blood circulation. By not having shoes on at home, people can release the pressure on their feet, which helps keep them healthy.

Another reason to avoid wearing shoes at home is to keep the floors of your house cleaner. As the bottom of our shoes collect dust and germs outside, wearing them in the house is unclean. For those who want to keep their carpets clean so that they can lay or sit down on them comfortably, not having shoes on at home works well.

People who come to Japan often find the country very healthy and clean. If they want to bring these good traits to their countries, they should start practicing our custom of not having shoes on at home.

！ここがポイント

このタイプのライティングをすると，「理由を３つ挙げなければいけない」と思っている学習者がいますが，その型で展開しにくい場合はそうする必要はありません．むしろ，たとえ一生懸命捻り出しても，「ああ，この３つ目の理由は無理矢理捻り出したんだな」と気づかれてしまえば，読み手は退屈になるし，試験答案であれば，点数は低くなります．Sample Answer では２つ理由を挙げていますが，その前に第１パラグラフで，慣習を別の共同体に根づかせることが難しいことだと断り書きを入れ，第２パラグラフでは室内でも靴を履く文化がある人たちに理解を見せたうえで，それでも自論に理があるという構成で展開しています．大事なのは，自分の思考が相手にわかるように明確な構成で書くことであって，思考が枠に制限されるのであればその枠を取り払ってしまったほうが良いものが書けるはずです．

訳　それぞれの共同体には異なる慣習（古くからのならわし）や慣例（世間のしきたり）があり，それらの多くはそれぞれの場所での必要性に基づいて生き残ってきたものだ．それゆえに，そういうならわしやしきたりを他の共同体に持ち込むのは容易なことではない．例えば，寒い地域の人々は暖かい地域で生まれた慣行の多くを取り入れることはできない．デンマークやフィンランドの人がアロハシャツを１年中着ていることなど不可能だ．それでもやはり，自分が生まれ育った日本の１つの慣行は他の国々に行き渡ってほしいと願っている．それは，家の中に入る前に靴を脱ぐことだ．

西欧諸国の多くの人は家の中でも靴を履いている．そうすることは私たちが店や銀行やオフィスの建物内では靴を履いているのと同じで，彼らにとっては自然なことなのかもしれない．そうだとしても，私は家の中では靴を履かない慣行を実践するほうがよいと考えている．

家の中で靴を履かない１つの理由は，足を長時間圧迫しないほうがよいからである．靴を履いている時，両足はきつい空間のなかに押し込められていて，その結果血の巡りが悪くなる．靴を家では履かないことで，足にかかる圧力を緩めることができ，それは健康につながる．

家の中で靴を履かないもう１つの理由は，家の床をより清潔に保つためである．私たちの靴は外の埃やばい菌を集めるので，そういう靴を家の中で履いているのは清潔ではない．カーペットを清潔に保って，快適にカーペットの上で横になったり，座ったりしたい人には，家の中で靴を履かないことでうまくいく．

日本にやってくる人々の中には日本がとても健康的かつ清潔だと思う人が多い．こういう良い特徴を自分の国に持ち込みたいと彼らが願うならば，まずは家の中で靴を履かないという我が国のならわしから実践してみたらよいと思う．

Give reasons for a preference

どちらに賛成かの理由を説明する TOEFL

Directions:

Read the question below. You have 30 minutes to plan, write, and revise your essay. Typically, an effective response will contain a minimum of 300 words.

以下の質問を読んで小論文を書きなさい. 構成を考え, 文章を書いて修正する時間は 30 分です. 通常, 効果的な回答は 300 ワード以上です.

Question:

Some people believe that college students should focus on studying. Others believe that they should spend more time for extracurricular activities such as sports, clubs, social gatherings, volunteering, or internships.

Which do you prefer? Support your answer with specific details.

大学生は勉強に集中したほうがよいと考える人もいれば, スポーツ, クラブ, 社交, ボランティア, インターンシップなどの課外活動にもっと時間を割いたほうがよいと考える人もいる. あなたはどちらに賛成か. 具体的な内容で理由を説明しなさい.

Intro

- 与えられた prompt を自分の言葉で言い換える.
- どちらが大事なのか自分の立場を明らかにする.

Reason #1

- 第 1 の理由として「実生活のなかでの豊かな学び」には前提となる知識が要ることを述べる.
- 具体例を挙げる.
- 学校は幅広く知識を身につける場所と説く.

Reason #2

- 第 2 の理由として「学生の時以外まとまって勉強する時間はとれない」と述べる.
- 社会人が時間をとって勉強するのがいかに難しいかを述べる.

Conclusion

- 余計なことは書かず，上に挙げた 2 つの理由を少し違う表現を使いながらまとめる.

Learning new things is very important for everyone. Learning can be done either through course work or through real life. When it comes to college students, however, the former is more important. Let me explain why I think this way.

First, not many students can learn only by experiencing. To understand what an experience means to them, they must have certain background knowledge. If you went to the Louvre Museum in Paris without any knowledge of art or history, for example, you could not fully enjoy what this great museum offers. Through volunteer work, you could recognize that a large number of people all over the world are facing poverty. Without enough knowledge about the world, however, you wouldn't learn why they are poor or how they can escape such poverty. School is where students usually develop this type of knowledge. Therefore, before maximizing your real-life experiences, it is important to learn a wide range of knowledge at school.

Second, after they graduate, students won't be able to find time to study as intensively as they do while in school. Regardless of what kind of jobs they will have, they will all have to work many hours. I hear that an average business person in the United States works longer than eight hours on weekdays and four to five hours on weekends. They could study in their free time, but it will not be easy to do so when they are busy with their work. If students study full-time, they should devote themselves to the task for many hours and wasting too much time on other things seems unwise.

For these two reasons, I believe college students should consider studying to be their priority. They should not do other activities if it means they must cut down the time spent studying.

！ここがポイント

① 普通の人は「勉強も課外活動もどっちだって大事だ」と思うでしょうが、「どちらでもよい」できちんとした答案を作るのは難しいと思います。　一方を選んで、「もう一方には……と考える人もいるだろうが」というのをどこかに述べるほうがまとまった答案に仕上がるはずです。IELTSもTOEFLもどちらを選ぶかではなく、一方を選んだ後、どれだけ論を展開できるかを測ろうと思っていて出題しているのですから。

訳 新しいことを学ぶことは誰にとっても重要だ。学ぶことは授業課題を通じてでも、日常生活からでもできる。ただ、大学生に限って言えば、前者の学びのほうがより重要だ。以下、なぜそう考えるかを示す。

まず、すべての学生が体験だけで学びが得られるわけではないからだ。ある経験が自分にとって持つ意味を理解するには、ある程度の背景知識が要る。美術や歴史の知識が皆無でパリのルーヴル美術館に行っても、この素晴らしい美術館が提供するものを十分に味わうことはできないだろう。ボランティア活動を通じて、世界中の多くの人が貧困に直面していることを学ぶことがあるかもしれない。だが、世界に関する十分な知識がなければ、なぜ彼らが貧しいのか、どうしたら貧困から抜け出せるのかまで学ぶことはできないだろう。学校は学生が日常的にこの種の知識を高める場所である。それゆえに、実地経験を積む前に、学校で幅広い知識を身につけることが重要だ。

次に、卒業後、学生は学校にいるときほど集中的に勉強することができない。職種に関わりなく、彼らは毎日長時間働かなくてはいけない。聞くところによれば、アメリカの平均的な会社員は平日には8時間以上、休日には4-5時間働くそうだ。空いた時間に勉強することは可能ではあるが、仕事で忙しい時にそうすることは簡単なことではない。もし、フルタイムの学生ならば、長時間勉強に自分自身を捧げるのは彼らの権利であり、他のことに時間を浪費するのは賢いとは思えない。

これら2つの理由から、大学生は学業を優先することを考えたほうがよいと私は思う。勉強をする時間を切り詰めなくてはならないような活動ならしないほうがよい。

Section 8

賛成理由／反対理由を説明する TOEFL

Directions:

Read the question below. You have 30 minutes to plan, write, and revise your essay. Typically, an effective response will contain a minimum of 300 words.

以下の質問を読んで小論文を書きなさい. 構成を考え, 文章を書いて修正する時間は 30 分です. 通常, 効果的な回答は 300 ワード以上です.

Question:

Do you agree or disagree with the following statement?

Financial management should be taught at school.

Use specific reasons and examples to support your answer.

あなたは次の意見に賛成ですか, それとも反対ですか.
財務管理は学校で教えられるべきである.
具体的な理由と例を挙げて, あなたの選択を説明しなさい.

Intro

 ・financial management を学校で子どもに教えることに対してどう思うか，自分の立場を明らかにする．

Definition

 ・自分の考える financial management を定義する．

Reason #1

 ・「お金の使い方を考えることは自分の夢や目標の実現を真剣に考えることに役に立つ」と主張する．

Reason #2

 ・「詐欺に遭わないために financial management の知識は重要」と述べる．

Conclusion

 ・ピリオド代わりに簡潔にまとめる．

Some people may disagree, but in my opinion, it is a good idea for schools to provide students with financial management courses, as long as students are given enough time to learn fundamental academic subjects.

Some people may associate financial management as skills necessary for millionaires and insist that it should not be taught in school because of that. Managing money does not always mean living a luxurious life while making a huge amount of money you didn't earn. It also refers to how you should save the money you earn from work. I strongly believe that the latter meaning, and not the former one, has to be taught explicitly in school.

Students should learn to save money or use it after careful planning, whether it is the money they get from their parents or that from a part-time job. For example, they may stop wasting money on little things like drinks and snacks, in order to purchase something they really want—such as a guitar to form a band with their friends or a trip to broaden their perspectives. Practicing money management skills like this naturally helps students think about what they want to do in the future and how they can accomplish it.

In addition, we have more and more crimes targeting people without financial knowledge. They are easily deceived by the stories criminals make up and as a result lose large amounts of money. In fact, a friend of mine lost most of her money investing in a start-up IT company, innocently believing that she could make the money back five times over within a couple of years. If school children learn how to not be deceived by such schemes, they, and potentially their parents, might be saved.

Teaching children financial management skills seem to have more advantages than disadvantages.

!■ ここがポイント

☞ こういう prompt だと，自分は「お金とか数字とか経済とかダメ．日本語でもわからない」と考えることを放棄してしまう学習者もいるようです．しかし，ライティングで必要なのは，経済についての専門知識でなく，与えられた課題に関して，考えを論理的に展開していく英語力です．Sample Answer のように，financial management を自分なりに定義しながら，論を展開していけば特別な財政や経済についての知識はまるでなくても書けるはずです．

訳 反対する人もいるかもしれないが，個人的には，基本的な教科学習に十分な時間が与えられている限りは，学校が生徒に財務管理の授業を提供するのは良いことだと思う．

財務管理を大金持ちに要求されるスキルと考え，そのため学校で教えるのはよくないと主張する人もいるかもしれない．お金を管理するということは自分が稼いだことのない巨額のお金を作りながら贅沢三昧の生活を送ることをかならずしも意味しない．それは，どのように自分が働いて稼いだお金を貯めるのかも意味する．私は前者ではなく後者の意味でのお金の管理に関しては学校できちんと教えたほうがよいと強く思う．

学生は親からもらったお金であれ，アルバイトで得たお金であれ，計画的に貯めたり，使ったりできるようになったほうがよい．例えば，友人とバンド活動をするためのギターや見聞を広げるための旅費といった本当に欲しいものを買うために，飲み物や軽食といったちょっとした出費を抑えるようになるとよい．このような財務管理を実際にやってみることは当然自分が将来やりたいことはなにか，それをどう実現するのかを生徒が考えるのに役立つ．

加えて，財政の知識がない人をターゲットにした犯罪が増えている．彼らは簡単に犯罪者がでっちあげた話に騙され，結果としてたくさんのお金を失う．事実，友人の1人は数年後にお金が5倍になって戻ってくるという話を信じて，IT ベンチャー企業に財産の大半を投資して失った．もし，学校が子どもにこういうたくらみに騙されない方法を教えるならば，子どもたちだけでなく両親も救われるのではないか．

子どもに財務管理を教えることは悪いことよりも良いことのほうが多いように思える．

「選んだもの」と「選んだ理由」を述べる TOEFL

Directions:

Read the question below. You have 30 minutes to plan, write, and revise your essay. Typically, an effective response will contain a minimum of 300 words.

以下の質問を読んで小論文を書きなさい. 構成を考え, 文章を書いて修正する時間は 30 分です. 通常, 効果的な回答は 300 ワード以上です.

Question:

If you could travel back in time to interview a famous person from history, what person would you like to meet?

Use specific reasons and details to support your answer.

もしタイムスリップして歴史上の有名人にインタビューできるとしたら, 誰に会ってみたいか. 答えるに当たってははっきりとした理由と詳細を述べなさい.

Who she/he is

- 歴史上の有名人を1人選ぶ.
- それがどんな人なのか簡潔に説明する.

What she/he did

- その人物の業績を述べる.
- その中で自分にとっていちばん大切／重要と思われる点は何かを考える.

What you would ask

- どんなことを相手にたずねたいか, 質問を列挙する.
- なぜそれらの質問をしたいかを説明する.

If I could go back to any time in the past, I would go to England 40 years ago and talk with John Lennon. John Lennon was a member of the internationally recognized British pop band, The Beatles. Lennon wrote some beautiful songs before and after the band was dissolved. Many people all over the world remember his songs such as *Yesterday*, *Let It Be*, *Strawberry Fields Forever*, and *Across the Universe*.

One of his most world-renowned songs is *Imagine*, which he wrote in 1971. He wrote this song one year after The Beatles split. It has been quoted or played in many movies, TV shows, and even school textbooks. One of the reasons this song has been loved by many people for ages is its lyrics. The lyrics are full of Lennon's wishes, as an idealist, for world peace.

If I had a chance to speak with Lennon, I would like to hear about why he wrote this song, what it meant to him, and how much of it was made by his wife's, Yoko Ono's, influence. There have been a lot of books or documentaries about him, so reading them might suggest how he would answer such questions. Having said that, I would like to hear the answers directly from him. Also, if possible, I would like to ask him how he feels about the world as it is today. I would love to know how the world today would look to Lennon, given the many ongoing conflicts between countries, cultures, and religions, such as those in Ukraine, Hong Kong, Afghanistan, or Palestine. Also, how would he feel about the United Kingdom and the United States now? Would he be disappointed, or would he keep believing that his wish will come true someday? After getting his answer to these questions, I would ask him to sing *Imagine* for me.

⚑ ここがポイント

👉 こういった prompt が頻繁に TOEFL に出題されることはおそらくない気がしますが，仮に出題された場合，自由に書いて構いません．ただし，自分なりの構成をはっきりさせること，自分が選んだ人物の描写と自分がその人物を選ぶ理由（＝インタビューする相手にたずねたいこと）をうまく結びつけて書けるかがライティングの質にかかわってきます．

訳 もし，私が過去のどの時点にでも戻ることができるならば，私は 40 年前のイギリスに行って，John Lennon と話をします．John Lennon は世界的に有名なイギリスのポップバンド，The Beatles のメンバーです．Lennon はたくさんの美しい歌を The Beatles の解散前も解散後も書きました．『Yesterday』，『Let It Be』，『Strawberry Fields Forever』，『Across the Universe』といった彼の曲は世界中の人々の心の中に残っています．

世界的に有名な歌のひとつに 1971 年に彼が書いた『Imagine』があります．この曲は彼が The Beatles 解散の 1 年後に書いたものです．この歌は多くの映画やテレビ番組，学校の教科書にも引用されています．長い間多くの人にこの歌が愛されている理由の 1 つは歌詞にあります．その歌詞には，理想主義者である Lennon の平和への願いがあふれています．

もし，私が Lennon と話す機会があったら，私はなぜ彼がこの歌を書いたのか，彼にとってこの歌はどういう意味をもつのか，どれだけ彼の妻 Yoko Ono の影響でできたものなのかを聞きたいです．彼についてのたくさんの本やドキュメンタリー映画があるので，そういったものを調べれば彼がどのように答えるのか想像はつくのかもしれません．それでも，彼から直接答えを聞きたいです．そして，もし可能ならば，彼が現在の世界をどう思うのかをたずねてみたいです．ぜひ，いまもウクライナや香港，アフガニスタン，パレスチナで起こっていることのような異なる国家や文化，宗教の間で戦争が絶え間なく起こっている現状を前にして，Lennon にとって世界はどう見えるのかを知りたいのです．また，彼は今のイギリスやアメリカをどう思うか？　彼はがっかりするのか，それとも自分の願いがいつかは叶うと信じ続けるのだろうか？　これらの質問への答えが得られたら，『Imagine』を歌ってくれるようにお願いしたいです．

Chapter 1 センテンスを組み立てる

Chapter 2 センテンスをつなげる

Chapter 3 文章をまとめる

著者略歴

石井洋佑 （いしい・ようすけ）

外国語辞書・語学書の編集，シカゴ郊外の公立高校勤務，留学相談や企業研修のカリキュラム作成などを経験後，現在は複数の教育機関で勤務する傍ら，語学書の執筆をしている．University of Central Missouri で MA-TESL（英語教授法修士）取得．『論理を学び表現力を養う 英語スピーキングルールブック』『ネイティブなら小学生でも知っている会話の基本ルール』（テイエス企画），『ゼロから覚醒 はじめよう英作文』（かんき出版），『はじめての TOEIC® L&R テストきほんのきほん』（スリーエーネットワーク），『「意味順」で学ぶ英会話』（JMAM）などの著書がある。

著書一覧　https://booklog.jp/users/yosukejishii/

15の論理展開パターンで攻略する
英文ライティング

2024年4月30日　初版第1刷発行

著　者——石井洋佑
　　　　　©2024 Yosuke Ishii
発行者——張　士洛
発行所——日本能率協会マネジメントセンター
　　　　　〒103-6009　東京都中央区日本橋2-7-1　東京日本橋タワー
　　　　　TEL 03(6362)4339(編集)／03(6362)4558(販売)
　　　　　FAX 03(3272)8127(編集・販売)
　　　　　https://www.jmam.co.jp/

装　丁——冨澤　崇（EBranch）
イラスト—いけがみますみ
英文校閲—Michael McDowell
本文DTP—清水裕久（Pesco Paint）
印刷所——三松堂株式会社
製本所——三松堂株式会社

本書の内容に関するお問い合わせは、2ページにてご案内しております。

ISBN 978-4-8005-9206-4　C3082
落丁・乱丁はおとりかえします。
PRINTED IN JAPAN

「意味順」で学ぶ英会話

田地野 彰 監修　中川 浩・石井 洋佑 著

A5 変判　176 頁

注目のメソッド「意味順」の【だれが】【する（です）】【だれ・なに】【どこ】【いつ】を覚えて、英語にとても大事な語順感覚を習得！
簡単なことでもスッと口から出てこない英語が、この本で練習すればパッと組み立てて話せるようになります。
本書の特徴は、

1. STEP 1「文法を学ぶ」──これだけできれば大体話せる、英会話に絶対必要な文法事項に特化して掲載。意味順BOXにあわせた文の組み立てポイントを解説
2. STEP 2「会話を見てみよう」──自然で簡単な会話例で、STEP1で習った文法事項の使い方を学び、音声ガイドに合わせて英語の語順を体得
3. STEP 3「会話をしてみよう」──STEP 1やSTEP 2で習った表現を会話の中で使う練習。話し手として、相手とどう話すかを考えながら実践

「やり直し英語」にも最適な「意味順」でリアルな英会話を学びましょう。

日本能率協会マネジメントセンター